PREFACE

My father, R. S. Roseberry, wanted me to prepare his autobiography for publication and gave me the typescript and his permission to do it my way. I wanted to honor his wishes, but delayed for several years, because it seemed such an awesome task. After encouragement from Dr. K. Neill Foster, Executive Vice President/Publisher of Christian Publications; Dr. Paul Alford, President of Toccoa Falls College; and Rev. David Kennedy, Assistant Vice President of Division of Overseas Ministries (DOM), I finally felt free to go ahead.

This book could not have become a reality without the prayers of many friends and the technical help and collaboration of my husband, Ralph Herber. I appreciate the time, many helpful suggestions and input of Dr. Harold L. Herber. Our friend, Mr. Mike Kovak helped tremendously in obtaining and setting up the computer and collaborating in the production of the typescript.

Part of my father's preface to his autobiography beautifully sums up his spirit and his life.

"*Crossing Frontiers With Christ* has been very real to me from the day we crossed over the boundary to an unknown and forbidden land, French

West Africa. Others who had crossed that boundary at the close of the nineteenth century were turned back. Their goal was the same—Timbuctoo and the Soudan—where the messengers of Christ had never trod. It was given to us who followed those first pioneers to enter that mysterious city on the Sahara Desert.

"However, the greatest 'frontier' I ever crossed was out of 'self' into the 'fullness of Christ.' This fullness of the Spirit continued to be the constant supply and enabling to overcome the obstacles of the flesh and to stand until the Light had penetrated many parts of that unknown land."

This book is dedicated to the memory of my father and his heroic band of pioneers.

—Ruth Herber

FOREWORD

I consider it a real honor to be asked to write this foreword for the book on the life of Rev. Robert S. Roseberry, one of the greatest pioneer missionaries of the twentieth century. In my earliest recollections of missionaries I recall hearing his name as a leader in opening French West Africa to the preaching of the gospel. One missionary statesman called Mr. Roseberry, "The David Livingston of West Africa."

When on the various occasions I heard him speak, I admired him greatly. I became more personally acquainted with him during his latter years when he was retired in DeLand, Florida. Even when he was over eighty years old, he was always ready to go anywhere when asked to speak on world missions.

He was a dynamic leader who was elected chairman of the large French West Africa field of The Christian and Missionary Alliance during a time when that field encompassed what is today eight different nations. As most outstanding leaders tend to be, some considered him to be autocratic even to the point of being dictatorial at times. But this was necessary in order to penetrate into vast areas of Satan's territory.

Many of his immediate predecessors died while preaching the gospel to various tribes. His own partner, Rev. David Muir died of Black Water Fever and Mr. Roseberry had to bury him when he did not even have sufficient wood to build a coffin. In his book, *The Niger Vision,* Mr. Roseberry describes the challenge which lay before him this way:

> *The Djallon Mountains began to loom up closer. What lay beyond the mountain range? The great Niger Valley! Would we be permitted to reach it, or would we be turned back as the early pioneers had been? What food for reflection.*

But he did pioneer it, opening the way for others to follow.

During these years he had several men working closely with him who were great missionaries in their own right. One of these men, Rev. Michael Kurlack was never in the limelight but was described by others as "the man who produced great results behind the scene." Mr. Kurlack's daughter Peggy married Dr. David Harvey. They spent a number of years in French West Africa. Dr. Harvey is presently a professor in World Missions at Toccoa Falls College.

Another great missionary, Rev. J. Clyde Ritchey, did not serve directly under Mr. Roseberry, but was in France preparing to go to the Ivory Coast when Mr. Roseberry came home to retire. Mr. Ritchey spent 45 years in missionary activity in the Ivory Coast. He says of Dr. Roseberry:

> *Some men are plodders, but a few are striders, like Robert Roseberry. When West Africa opened to Protestant missions at the close of World War I,*

Robert was among the first who crossed from Sierra Leone into West Africa. He had a vision to penetrate the heartland of Africa with the gospel of Christ. He saw that vision come true as he stood at the head of the Niger river near the fabled city of Timbuctou.

He was a big man who left big tracks in the sands of time. The full extent of his ministry will only be known in eternity. "Bishop" Roseberry, as he was known, was a big man with a big vision that would culminate in seeing thousands of strong churches being founded and hundreds of thousands of people who today bless this great man of history.

Many of Mr. Roseberry's experiences were recorded in two books he wrote. The first, *Niger Vision,* published in 1934, had a great impact upon Clyde Ritchey's life. The second book, *The Soul of French West Africa,* was published in 1947. Roseberry began his autobiography, *Crossing Frontiers With Christ,* which his daughter Mrs. Ruth Herber completed. She gives a new perspective on the missionary activity of some of those early pioneers of faith.

Mrs. Herber, with her husband Ralph, spent a lifetime serving the Lord Jesus Christ in French West Africa. It is interesting to note the input of a daughter who admired her father and mother. Their lives influenced her to commit her life totally to Christ to reach the world for Him.

7

Edith Roseberry, who Mr. Roseberry married after they had each gone to the field as single missionaries, wrote a booklet entitled, *Kansas Prairies to African Forests,* published in 1957. Helen Martin, in the foreword of this booklet, states:

> *A great many of the missionaries in French West Africa are indebted to Mrs. R. S. Roseberry— lovingly known to us as Madame Roseberry—for our first introduction to missionary life. Her quiet, deep spirituality created a climate of rest and peace wherever she happened to be—whether in the busy life at headquarters in Kankan, or visiting us in the bush in the far eastern hinterland.*

To review the two previous books by Roseberry as well as the manuscript of this book have challenged me as I prepared this foreword. What these early missionaries accomplished in the spreading of the gospel and planting of the church is remarkable.

It is my hope this book will inspire many young men and women. Even though the conditions are different, the cost is the same—total commitment of their lives, regardless of the cost, to world evangelism to bring back the King!

—Dr. Paul L. Alford

TABLE OF CONTENTS

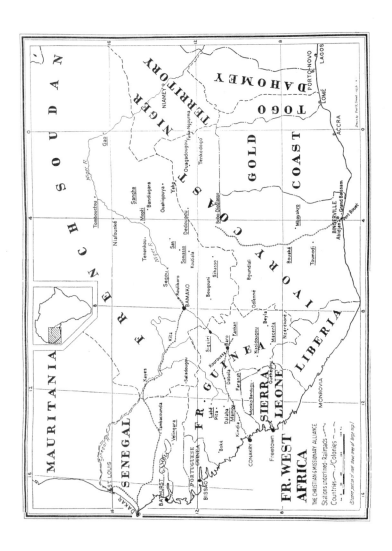

MAURITANIA

FRENCH SOUDAN

Tombouctou
Niafounké
Gao

Sangha
Bandiagara
Mopti
Ouahigouya
Yako
Ouagadougou
Fada-Ngourma
Tenkodogo
Dedougou
Bobo-Dioulasso

NIGER TERRITORY
NIAMEY

Tenenkou
San
Somasso
Koutiala

DAHOMEY
PORTO-NOVO
LAGOS
LOMÉ
TOGO
ACCRA

GOLD COAST

IVORY COAST

Mbayakro
Grand Bassam
BINGERVILLE
Abidjan Port Bouet
Toumodi
Bouaké

Sagou
Koulikoro
BAMAKO
Bougouni
Sikasso
Odienné
Boundiali
Beyla
Macenta
N'zérékoré

SENEGAL
ST LOUIS
DAKAR
BATHURST
GAMBIA
Tambacounda
Vélingara

FR. GUINEA
Kita
Siguiri
Kita
Faro
Kankan
Kankan
Kouroussa
Kissidougou
LIBERIA
MONROVIA

PORTUGUESE GUINEA
BISSAO
Labé
Pita
Dalaba
Mamou
Kindia
CONAKRY
Baki
Faranah
Dabola

SIERRA LEONE
Freetown
Menka-Bendugu
Gberia
Kabala

Kayes
Kita
Satadougou

Niger R.

FR. WEST AFRICA
THE CHRISTIAN & MISSIONARY ALLIANCE
Stations underlined; Railroads ↝
Countries _____ Colonies _____
(Crosses section of inset shows area of larger map)

Chapter 1

THE LIFTING OF THE CLOUD

It was early one morning in July of 1942, when the huge amphibian plane took off from New York Harbor heading for Natal, Brazil. Its final destination—Liberia, West Africa. There would be two brief stops, one at Miami and the other at Trinidad, West Indies. Not many passengers occupied the seats in the two spacious cabins. A crew of twelve young men kept everything running smoothly and hot meals were served regularly at three tables for four.

For Rev. R. S. Roseberry and Rev. George Stadsklev, the two missionary men on board, it was adequate in every way except for sleeping. They hunted up some cushions to lay on the rough ammunition crates in the cargo area and settled in for the long flight back to West Africa. They were joined later at Natal by two government officials on their way to Liberia.

World War II was at its peak. German submarines had made the Atlantic Ocean unsafe for travel by ship. The Elder Dempster Line, used by most missions for their overseas trips, had lost forty-four of its ships. As the eighty-ton Clipper sped through the darkness thousands of feet above the ocean depths, the two men rejoiced in God's provision.

The drone of the four huge engines half lulled the men to sleep, but at the same time their minds were preoccupied with thoughts of families left behind, children they would miss and the uncertainties of the future.

Their destination might well mean suffering and loneliness, because West Africa was under the control of Nazi Germany through the puppet regime of Vichy, France. Two missionaries had already been thrown into jail on a false charge and another was in danger. A missionary from a sister mission had died in jail for answering a question from a man seeking a way out of the country.

For Roseberry, it was a lifting of the cloud. Pearl Harbor had caused a cancellation of his return to West Africa in 1941. Since no way of return had opened up, he had accepted a position on the staff of Simpson Bible School on the west coast teaching Bible and Missions, a ministry he dearly loved. *He couldn't have known that during this interim he would influence several young people who later joined him in West Africa.*

"How did I get here?" Roseberry wondered as the plane bored steadily eastward. He went through the events of the past week again in his mind.

Dr. A. C. Snead, Foreign Secretary of the

14

Christian and Missionary Alliance, had accompanied him to Washington D.C. for an interview at the request of the U.S. Government. Only Roseberry was ushered into the office of the Colonel of Section Q at the Pentagon.

The Colonel told of the worsening military situation in the Atlantic and Europe. If Germany could control Africa too, it would give them a strategic advantage and they would put a submarine base in Dakar to control the Atlantic shipping lanes. The Pentagon wanted information about the inland and coastal areas. In other words, Roseberry was being recruited as an informant!

Roseberry stirred uneasily on his crate bed as the scenes of that interview came flooding across his mind. He had not wanted to accept the proposition and the Colonel was disappointed.

"Where is your patriotism?" he asked angrily.

"I am a patriot, but I am also a missionary and could not do what you ask of me," Roseberry quickly replied.

However, Washington doesn't give up easily. He remembered the government aide assigned to accompany him every moment. He took him out to a training camp in the country where they would be known by their first names only. Their mail would come through a special Washington address and there would be special classes about codes for relaying information, such as types of troop deployment, troop strength and modern warfare in general. It would end with a trip to Aberdeen proving grounds to see the big guns fired. The penalty for failure to comply with orders was $10,000! Roseberry had to make a decision. He could not follow this plan.

After one day at the camp, he found transportation back to Washington. Back at the hotel he was told to go to a certain room and knock on the door. He did so and met a man who told him little, but got him back to New York. The plane that would take him back to Africa would leave in a few days.

The U.S. Government officials realized that even if the government could not count on receiving information from him, he would be a means of encouraging the Free French. Roseberry, known for some twenty years as the Mission Director, could convey to the beleaguered officials that America was coming to their aide.

It was important that Roseberry get back to the mission field to encourage the small band of missionaries living and working in distressing circumstances, but he could not put himself in a position where he had to deceive and lie. That would bring his ministry to an end and the missionary endeavor would be jeopardized.

On the eve of his departure, Dr. H. M. Shuman, then President of the Christian and Missionary Alliance, came to his room and encouraged him to follow his conscience.

There would be loneliness, since there could be no possibility for his wife to join him for over a year. There would be hardship and the year ahead would not be easy, but Roseberry had long ago learned to face the unknown future with faith and courage in God.

As Dr. Shuman prayed for him, he felt a surge of faith and strength in his spirit. The cloud was lifting, the way ahead was clear!

Chapter 2

RETURN TO WEST AFRICA

It was Saturday evening when the big seaplane and its strange cargo lifted off the coast of Brazil heading eastward toward the West Coast of Africa. The crew and passengers flew far above the German Wolf Pack through the night. Many wearisome hours later, they landed on Fisherman's Lake near Monrovia, Liberia. There were only a few dilapidated buildings for the care of passengers and cargo and the countryside looked wild and unkempt.

July marks the beginning of a long wet season—not exactly the time for an overland trek—so the men would travel by plane as far as possible.

They rode a tractor around bushes, through mud and water and grass fields with Roseberry on the back bumper, Stadsclev on a side fender and the officials on the hood. They were grateful to see the small plane that would take them inland to Robert's Field on the Firestone Rubber Plantation. It was a short flight over waving palm forests down onto the plantation field before the tropical night fell.

Two mosquito net-covered army cots stood on the veranda of the barracks to meet their needs for the night. No lights were allowed after six p.m. because of the danger of attack from above. There was heavy rain during the night, when ten U. S. planes tried to land. With the airfield barely visible, nine of the planes managed to land, but the tenth crashed into the sea. Several men were killed and others thrown into the water. One man was missing and others were badly injured.

The weather raised concern over the 200 miles the missionaries would have to travel inland to their final destination. They didn't know the route and had no supplies. They didn't know what God's provision would be, but committing themselves to His care, they fell asleep. Step by step, God would show His leading and His will.

When morning dawned, the two men poked their heads out from under the nets as a stranger walked up.

"Where are you going?" he asked

"We are going to French West Africa," Roseberry replied.

"Your name is Roseberry, is it not?" the man asked.

"And your name is Dibble, is it not?" asked Roseberry.

The men had met in 1928 as they crossed the ocean together. Dibble was oil inspector for Pan Air Company and had failed to get a flight out the previous day. He was the helper they needed.

Dibble introduced them to Mr. Davy, a spiritual

instructor and teacher for thousands of men working at the Firestone Rubber Plantation and general host for missionaries passing through. Davy took them in charge, got them supplies, hammocks and porters for transportation. Last of all, he located an interpreter and a map of the route where they could stay at Mission Stations of the World Evangelization Crusade.

July in Liberia is marked by frequent deluges of rain, turning streets into rivers in a short time. On the eve of their cross-country trek they realized how God had watched over them. God provided a miracle—a dry spell while they were traveling!

Each man was carried in a hammock, supported by two teams of four men, but going up hills, the men preferred to walk.
Mission stations stretching across Liberia were hospitality havens during the grueling trip and provided needed rest stops for the men and their porters. Hoping to take a more direct route to the Ivory Coast, George Stadsclev left the caravan, but later rejoined the party at Sarokole when the border guard refused to let him pass.

They received proper entry papers at Sarokole, which was the residence of the District Commissioner. They were also able to get a truck ride for eighteen miles, which saved a day's journey. A mission nurse joined the party to visit a village en route.

All went well until the car broke down just

before they reached a bridge. It seemed a good idea to push the car to get it started, but the bridge collapsed under the weight.

Roseberry fell into the river hitting his side on the truck fender, breaking some ribs. The nurse taped him up and after a day of rest, the trek continued. Along the way they found a supply of quinine sent by Pan Am after permission to export had been received. God knew how important quinine was to the missionaries.

Nearing the end of their journey, the small party reached the border and entered French territory. Guards in red turbans met and escorted them to the French government post at N'Zerekore, which was bristling with military troops. Officials received them and treated them well.

After completing the last lap of his journey to Kankan aboard a truck run by charcoal gas, Roseberry received a royal welcome at the Guinea Mission headquarters.

Being so isolated by the war, the missionaries were always grateful for news from the homeland and they wanted to share what had happened on their stations. The blessing of the Lord had been on them and they were ready to push ahead as doors opened.

Chapter 3

SINKING VALLEY

The French colonies had been closed to Protestant Missions until 1918. The colonies were a huge block of spiritual darkness penetrated in some areas by the Roman Catholic Church and Islamic missionaries.

Who was this man who led in the opening of French West Africa to the gospel? He was known as RSR, sometimes, Roseberry, but he was more often called "the Bishop" by the early group of missionaries who followed his leadership.

I knew him well, for he was my father. He was a spiritual giant and leader—a great influence on my life and many others as well. Let him tell in his own words, a bit of his background.

"Sinking Valley, nestled away in the Western Pennsylvania mountains, was settled by emigrants from Scotland and Northern Ireland. This valley, heavily wooded with white oak, was cleared for farmland in the late 19th century," Roseberry said. "Lead mines in the valley helped supply lead for George Washington's army. Two small villages, Skelp and Arch Springs, were the sites for the Post

Office and small stores servicing the valley families.

"The Presbyterian church at one end of the valley and a Lutheran church on the other tended to the spiritual needs of the people. A Union Sunday School, representing different faiths, met in a country school house near Skelp.

"Into this valley came a branch of the Roseberry family from Scotland and North Ireland. They were Presbyterian in faith and were faithful to the tenets of the church. Great Grandfather Robert Roseborough, buried in the Arch Springs cemetery in 1850, was joined many years later by my grandparents Isaac and Martha Roseberry.

"Isaac and Martha had six children, the youngest was Robert, my father. The boys became famous as wood choppers as they cleared the land. In a timber bee, the brothers had to be held back or they would cut off their section before the others.

"The children were brought up in all the strict disciplines of the church. Family prayers and the Word of God laid a foundation in each of their lives. When I visited their homes in later years, I was impressed with the fervent prayers of these men.

"My mother, Margaret Watt, came from different stock. Her mother was a Quaker and her father a coal operator in the town of Gallitzen. Since he was addicted to drink, his holdings in the coal industry disappeared, leaving no inheritance.

"When my mother came to Sinking Valley to help her aunt on a farm, she and my father met.

Roseberry at the Missionary Training Institute, Nyack, New York, 1908.

Roseberry and Edith Plattenburg wed in the Chapel at
Mayasa, Sierra Leone in 1914.

Roseberrys with co-workers in Kurankoland, Sierra Leone.

Bush travel in the forest country of Sierra Leone.

Lewis and Clifford Ryan lead the first C. & M.A. missionary expedition into French West Africa, 1918.

Roseberry, his wife Edith and daughter Ruth return from furlough in 1922 to resume the chairmanship of the Mission at Kankan, Guinea.

After a proper courtship they were married.

"My father purchased property in the village of Skelp and I was born in that humble home on November 22, 1883. I can still remember hearing the gentle noise of the small creek running over the rocks, that lulled me to sleep at night."

"Five boys and three girls were born to Robert and Margaret. As the children grew, it was time to utilize the united strength of the family. The family moved to another farm and the children went to work, learning the art of farming.

"There was no modern machinery. The work was done the hard way—by sheer strength and grit," Roseberry said. "Each of the five boys was expected to do his share of the work. There was no warming of hands in pockets for lack of gloves. Father would say, 'Get those hands out of your pockets.' The three girls shared in the chores of the home."

With five boys isolated on a farm and no communication facilities but their feet, it was a situation ripe for an internal explosion. A letter from my father included this account: "We found a pack of cards in a lumber camp and soon learned to play Eucher, Seven Up and what not. We used grains of corn for antes. Fortunately mice ate up the pack which we hid in the barn so Daddy wouldn't see it!

"Another part of our hidden arsenal was a long barreled revolver. My brother Charley would shoot fish in shallow water. Daddy saw the hole in the fish's head and asked, 'What is that?' Charley told him that was where we killed it. The secret was safe! When we were older we practiced shooting on the front gable of the bake house, which did not improve its looks. As soon as we could hold a long barreled muzzle loading gun, we tramped the surrounding forests for game. Skunks and foxes were plentiful and their pelts provided ready cash. Each boy, as he became strong enough for the sport, was taught by his elder."

A crisis came that could have changed the boys lives. "Father was ill for days and did not expect to recover," Roseberry said. "He and Mother talked over what to do with the boys. They though it would be best to put them out with different people to work for their keep. The family doctor was called. He looked the patient over and then said in a rough voice, 'Bob, you are just lazy! Get up and go to work! Don't let your wife do all the work.' Father was so angry at being called lazy, he got up and went to work and the illness soon disappeared. The family was kept together and the Lord prospered us. We grew to manhood in the atmosphere of a home that stood for righteousness and integrity."

Chapter 4

EARLY HOME INFLUENCES

Roseberry felt the strong influence of family as he was growing up.

"The Bible was read just before bedtime and then everyone kneeled in prayer, seeking divine help and protection. Father met the Lord as a young man in a log cabin in the woods when he was felling trees. He did not always walk in the light, but down deep in his heart was a desire to follow the Lord," Roseberry said.

"In times of great emergency the family was called to prayer. In 1899, the Johnstown flood affected many areas of Pennsylvania. The creek running by our little home was becoming a raging torrent that threatened to carry our home from its foundation. The family was called to prayer. Water was coming into the cellar and the situation looked bad. Father urged mother to take the children to higher ground, but we all stayed together. By morning, the flood had crested and was receding. We had been delivered!

"A godly aunt, Ellen Roseberry, was also a great influence on my life. Blinded in an epidemic of small pox, she found the Lord as her Savior in a school for the blind in Philadelphia. She would gather us children around her on Sunday evenings and tell us Bible stories. She would quiz us afterwards and we became familiar with the history of the Bible. Who can tell what a safeguard that was to us to know the Holy Scriptures from early childhood."

When he was nine years old, Roseberry attended evangelistic services in the little school house. He stood when the invitation was given, as did most of the family. Although he was considered too young to understand, he knew then that he was a sinner and in need of salvation.

Five years later, in the same school house, when his mother urged him to make a stand for the Lord, Roseberry went forward and expressed his desire to be a Christian. He did not understand the delivering power of the Spirit in His fullness then, but it was an anchor to keep him from yielding to the temptations that come to every young man.

After finishing his years in grade school, Roseberry decided to go to Indiana State Normal School in Pennsylvania and prepare to teach in public schools. After passing the Blair county examination for public school teaching, he was given a school in the valley, where he taught for two years. He planned to continue his training in Normal School, but the Lord had other work for him to do.

Chapter 5

THE HOLINESS BAND

For years a group of men and women from the Methodist church in Tyrone, Pennsylvania had banded together to pray for God's blessing. In that group was Mr. and Mrs. Frank Waring who had moved into the valley to engage in fruit growing. They began to attend the Union Sunday School and cottage prayer meetings and Mrs. Waring started to pray for a spiritual awakening in the valley. At one of the cottage meetings God's Spirit came on her in prayer and she "knew" that an awakening would take place.

Grace Waring's sister was an evangelist filled with the Holy Spirit and a burden to reach the lost. She was married to Doctor Baer of Camden, New Jersey. She was asked to come and hold meetings in the school house at Tyrone.

"I went the second night and was caught by the Spirit," said Roseberry. "Mrs. Baer came to me in her quiet, earnest way and asked if I was saved.

"I hope so," I said.

"She told me I could have the assurance of salvation. That was a new message to me and I went out a deeply wounded man that night. Those two weeks will live forever in my memory. I immediately became an active disciple of Christ and began to bear witness to the faith within me.

"Summer came and my brother Charles and I attended the Rocky Springs convention near Lancaster, Pennsylvania," Roseberry continued. "In our empty tent we bedded down on straw from a nearby barn. While there, we heard about the Missionary Training Institute at Nyack, New York. The Christian and Missionary Alliance workers were a great blessing to us.

"After the convention, my heart was still seeking a fuller experience. How well I remember the rendezvous with the Lord out in the forest under the spreading pine trees. There, alone with the Lord, I lifted my hands to heaven and cried, 'Lord, give me your power and I will go to the ends of the earth.' God was there and the covenant was made. I went out from that holy place with great quietness of soul. A few days later in the old school house, the Spirit of God came on me in prayer and confirmed my ministry."

When a conviction to prepare for the mission field began to fill Roseberry's heart, at first his father was not happy about his desire to go to Nyack. He said he needed Roseberry during his declining years. But he later yielded and gave his blessing.

Money saved from teaching school paid his first

two years of Nyack and Grace Waring paid for the third year. She had been used in praying down revival for the valley community and now she considered him her representative at the battle front.

He was to do pioneer work in the dark continent, but the vision was not clear all at once. There was just the strong conviction to follow Jesus and prepare for His service.

Chapter 6

NYACK ON THE HUDSON

Work at Indiana State Normal School was set aside as Roseberry turned his face toward the Missionary Training Institute at Nyack, New York. The direction and interest of his life had been changed forever.

The fall of 1906 marked a new experience at Nyack. The students were devoted to the Lord and fires for missions were kindled by returning missionaries every Friday evening. News of the Welsh Revival that had begun in 1904 was a challenge to the students, who in turn began asking God for revival. A young Welshman from Wales came and fanned the flame in song and message and revival came!

Classes were suspended and prayer, confession and testimony filled the hours for days. Some tried to leave the school, but were held by the invisible hand of the Lord. One student fled as far as the railroad station, but had to return and make his confession. He later became an evangelist.

The fires burned on and students were endued with power. They went to the ends of the earth to tell the news of salvation. At that time Dr. Simpson had a vision of a keyboard. The Lord told him to keep his hands off the keyboard because He was sending the gospel to all the world. The vision came true as vigorous societies sprang up and, with the power of the Spirit, entered into many lands with the message. Thousands of lost ones were brought into the fold.

"We cannot forget Dr. Simpson's lectures on 'Christ and the Bible' each Wednesday. He seemed like a prophet out of the Old Testament as he unfolded great truths of the Bible," Roseberry said. "Dr. Simpson also called the young men together and talked to them about personal victory over the lusts of the flesh. He said, 'You are going to the mission field. Can you trust Him for victory over the flesh?' His ministry was unique in many ways and we remembered these words years later when we found ourselves alone in Africa."

Other men of God, through instruction and counseling, also left their mark on the student body. W. C. Stevens, known for his rugged faith and stern discipline, led the young people in effective ways to study the Bible. When demonic forces tried to enter and break up the revival, he called students to united prayer while he faced and rebuked the enemy—and victory came!

Dr. Pardington was physically handicapped and often had to be helped down the cement walk to his house. But who could forget the hours spent with him? Students learned how to reckon themselves dead unto sin and alive unto righteousness. Godly teachers projected their lives and vision to men and women who in turn carried the message to the "regions beyond."

Time went by rapidly and when the years of training were over, Roseberry was one of the Commencement Day speakers. His heart burned within him as he spoke on the topic, "The Man Behind the Message." Preparation days were over— where would God lead him? Pioneer work called for full sacrifice and devotion, but the call was clear and he was ready.

Chapter 7

THE CALL OF THE SOUDAN

When the call for volunteers came from the Soudan Mission in Sierra Leone, Roseberry responded. Nineteen years before, a band of pioneers had gone into this area with the commission to open a way to the Niger River and from there, to push on to Timbuctoo in the Sahara Desert. What they found was an unsettled and primitive country.

Regardless of adverse conditions, nine men obtained a native canoe and started for the interior down the Rokel River. The first station was opened at Mabele and the second was at Robethel where a boy's school was constructed. They learned the Temne language. While the people were friendly, they were strong fetish worshippers and did not respond quickly to the gospel message.

Death soon invaded the ranks and within six months, five of the men had passed away. Malaria fever was deadly with no quinine to combat it. Other recruits came and they suffered also. Sierra Leone became known as the "white man's graveyard."

In spite of the adversities, by 1895 the mission had opened a base at Tibabadougou, about two days trek from the Niger River. They crossed over into French territory, but were never allowed to proceed. It was years before the dream of reaching Timbuctoo was realized.

When Roseberry and another young man arrived in Freetown in October of 1909, conditions had improved somewhat. Instead of long treks overland, they were able to ride part of the way on a freight train to the village of Makump.

"We set out with Pa Smitty (Howard Smith, superintendent of the mission) who had come to meet us," Roseberry said about that first trip. "The sun was hot and the road interminable as we traveled through thick bush. We passed by large rice fields soon to be harvested and had to learn to walk across poles that served for bridges. We did not have much baggage. Part of it was hauled by a makeshift cart pulled by oxen. The oxen died mysteriously on the way. Though the porters brought the tails to tell of the loss, no good explanation was given."

When the remaining band of missionaries met to plan their strategy for the future, it was decided that Roseberry would be teamed with a senior worker, David Muir, to open two new stations nearly sixty miles into the interior. After conference, the men arranged their baggage in sixty-pound loads, so that porters could carry it over the steep mountains ahead.

Thanksgiving Day provided a pleasant interlude at the station of Masambiri when Miss Grace Kennedy and Miss Edith Plattenburg served a traditional meal. *Little did Roseberry know that one day Edith Plattenburg would become his wife.*

The men set out again for the Belekwonke mountain looming ahead. A narrow path wound ever upward around gullies and through streams. The sun was hot and they made frequent rest stops. The days of walking seemed endless. At each village, Mr. Muir would give a short message on God's great plan of redemption.

It was twilight by the time they reached a small village at the edge of the forest where they would camp for the night. Weariness brought sleep in spite of the tom-toms that seemed to beat all night.
At journey's end there was no house waiting, so the men had to build their home. Funds were low and time could not be wasted on building an elaborate bungalow. Posts were put in the ground to support the roof of tall elephant grass and the sides were tied with woven palm fronds. That was it.

Their portable camp cots soon gave way and no lumber was available except the split boards cut out of the forest by African blacksmiths. Later the men learned how to use a pit saw, which required two men working together to pull and push the long saw up and down to cut the log. The results, however, were not much better.

Efforts to open a second out-station ended rather suddenly. The new house was off the ground on short pillars to escape the termites and the wood floor was laid down on floor beams, then covered with clay. The roof was the usual thatch. It seemed satisfactory until the fire in the small fireplace blazed up catching the roof on fire and turning the little home to ashes. Some kind people helped remove Roseberry's belongings and he rejoined Mr. Muir at the head station. This proved to be a timely move.

All seemed well when the men read the Word and prayed together one morning. But by noon David Muir had a high fever. When blood began to flow through his kidneys, they recognized the dreaded disease of black water fever, a complication of malaria. It was impossible to get outside help and although a messenger was sent to the nearest station, help did not arrive in time. The third day, David Muir's spirit took flight and Roseberry had the sad duty of wrapping his colleague's body in fiber mats which were encased with a few rough, hand-sawed boards. He laid him in a newly dug grave and another life was laid down. The response of the people had been meager.

"I traveled and preached in many villages, giving out the Word of Life," a burdened Roseberry wrote, "but the people in Kuranko land were slow to hear. I poured out my heart, but still no response. The mission had spent 20 years in Sierra Leone and yet there was no established church. What would it take to bring these people to God?

"My first term was about to close. I met for a last time of fellowship with the other missionaries during our Field Conference at the head station then turned my face toward the homeland and furlough.

"As I was about to leave, the big-eyed handicapped boy who had been my companion through different recent trials, came to me to say farewell. He was weeping and the parting was difficult. 'Loosebelly,' he said, 'you must not come back to this country when you return home—you will die out here. We would like to have you but you must not return.' I confess that I myself felt somewhat the same in the midst of the trouble, but Christ abiding within gives renewed courage. I comforted him, entrusted my dog to his care, and sent him back to his people."

In May of 1932, Roseberry journeyed back to Sierra Leone to encourage the small staff still working there. The trek was still by bush road or foot path, around mountains and through swamps and valleys.

Little had changed in the town where Roseberry had begun his career twenty-three years before, except for the crippled boy who had cooked for him. He was now a man, but they recognized each other at once. Overjoyed to be with his friend "Loosebelly" again, he wanted to go with him back to Kankan. He had not forgotten how to pray, but wanted to learn to read the Word of God. Roseberry couldn't take his friend, but left him in the care of the missionary couple at the next mission station, Mr. and Mrs. Montrose Waite. They would care for him.

One goal of this visit was to stand again at the grave of David Muir. As he stood there, Roseberry remembered that bitter and lonely moment of David's death. But now he was looking at it from a different perspective. He could see how in that darkest of hours, God had a plan and he could rejoice, for David's life had not been laid down in vain. There was now a line of mission stations reaching across the French Soudan from Baro in Guinea to Gao in the Sahara Desert. God's church was born and the goal inspired by Dr. Simpson's vision had been reached.

Chapter 8

LET THEM PASS

Roseberry's first furlough was a new and interesting experience. Teamed up in missionary conventions with such veteran missionaries as Mr. Christie of Tibet and Mr. Isaac Hess of China, he received new inspiration and courage to go on. While in the Rocky Springs convention near Lancaster, Pennsylvania, Dr. Simpson came and personally encouraged him and suggested he start looking for a wife. It was not easy, however, to find the will of the Lord for such an important matter in his life.

When it was time to return to Africa, Roseberry was teamed up with Mr. Ray Custer, an experienced carpenter, who was a great help in building mission stations and chapels. Together, they were appointed to re-open Tibabadougou, an inland post of the early pioneers. The old house had blown down and been rebuilt. The lonely graveyard in the tall reed grass told of the battle that had been waged. They repaired the old chapel near the village, but still the Kuranko people did not respond to the message.

Eighteen miles away, two pioneer ladies had

volunteered to re-open the station at Farandougou. Because the staff of workers had dwindled, Miss Edith Plattenburg and Miss Frutiger attempted this task alone. Roseberry and Custer made frequent trips to help the ladies in building and in evangelism. Less than a year later there were two weddings at the mission.

Roseberry had carried a box from the Ashley Alliance Church in Pennsylvania for Edith in his baggage. In it were new shoes, a complete outfit of personal clothing and white dress material with lace for trimming. Each article was wrapped in white tissue paper and tied with blue ribbon—a bride's trousseau!

Very shortly after their marriage Roseberry and Edith moved to headquarters at Makump to assume the chairmanship of the mission.

The smoldering embers of the faded vision to enter the French Soudan became a flame as World War I brought new conditions into being. At that time the leading nations of the world signed the St. Germain Treaty, which granted the right to all foreign missionaries to enter and carry on missionary work in all Mandate territories and colonies. Up to this time only French missionaries could enter French controlled regions.

Mr. Mitchell from the Sierra Leone staff had gone to Paris to interview the French government regarding permission to enter their territories. Hope ran high, but the reply was not favorable.

44

Later in the fall of 1917, three missionaries, Rev. and Mrs. A. E. Loose and Mrs. Graham were sailing for Sierra Leone via France when they met a French official, Mr Newry. He was head of the Department of Agriculture of French Guinea and promised to help them get an interview with officials in Conakry.

He was true to his word and when Roseberry and Loose went to Conakry, he took them to see Governor Monsieur Poiret. He received them kindly and was favorable to their entry into the French Colony as long as they would not employ force with existing religions.

The following mission conference decided it was time to advance into this great unevangelized territory. They appointed the two Ryan brothers, Clifford and Lewis, to attempt the long trip to French territory in the hope of finding a good location for the first mission station.

It was a long, hard journey. The country was wild and it took real courage and stamina to follow man-made trails through veritable jungles and over steep mountains. One of the men once stepped over what he thought was a log. When it started to move, he realized it was a boa constrictor moving away from under his feet!

Samory, the great Muslim conqueror, had devastated much of the land in his quest for Muslim converts. Deserted towns and broken down walls were testimony to his cruelty and ruthless ways. Village chiefs had been put on the alert for strangers, thinking that some troublesome Germans might sneak across the border and cause havoc.

The missionaries carried no guns and lived on the food they could get in villages they passed through. When they arrived, weary and hungry, at the border town of Moridugu unannounced, the village chief was startled and sent a message at once to the French administrator, who in turn sent a guard to interview the men. The guard had known the Ryan brothers back in Sierra Leone and reported back to the administrator that these were not spies, but American missionaries. The French official came to see for himself and wired Conakry. The word came back, "Let them pass!" The Soudan had been gained at last!

The Ryan brothers returned with the news after several months of travel and the missionary staff rejoiced.

"The homeland was electrified and offered to back us fully so we could extend our lines down the Niger River," Roseberry wrote. "We owe a great debt to Dr. A. C. Snead who promoted the advance in person. He counseled us to penetrate the cities, which proved to be the only course for a rapid advance into the territory."

Property in suburban areas was hard to obtain, while traders in the cities were always willing to sell concessions. A Ford car was sent to help in establishing mission stations throughout the Soudan. As they were established, reinforcements, as well as funds to buy property, came. It was God's time to advance.

Chapter 9

POSSESSING THE LAND

By 1919, the first station in French West Africa had become a reality. It was located on the border of the Niandan River which flowed into the Niger and was a straight shot to Bamako, the capitol of the French Soudan. The river provided the best way to go, since there was no linkage by road, train or plane in the 1900's. Roseberry and Lewis Ryan were sent to locate property on or near the river for necessary dwellings.

The people of Baro, a large provincial town a mile from the railway station, received them kindly enough, but they did not know the men or understand why they were there. The chief, Mpali, was reluctant to give them lodging or property until official permission was received from the Governor.

However, God had a plan.

They noticed some houses built outside the town and upon inquiring, found the owner, Isiaka Ba (Isaac the Great), who had moved there after being mistreated by the chief. He rented them his best house, an adobe brick dwelling with a thatch roof. As the staff of workers grew, they took over more and more huts.

Their search for property led them to a site outside the village under some spreading trees. It was actually the graveyard property, and many laws and much red tape hindered the purchase. Out of necessity, they decided to risk putting up temporary quarters. Two round huts with a connecting roofed passageway seemed to be a good idea. Lumber for the houses had to be cut out of the nearby forest.

The time for roofing coincided with seed sowing time for the farmers who were anxiously awaiting rains that didn't come. They looked at the unroofed houses of the missionaries and decided that God was holding up the rain until the work was done.

"Let's help them roof their houses so the rain may come on our land," they said.

Getting the water palm poles and suitable grass for thatch was a day's walk away, but the men of the village turned out with a will and the job was soon done. That night the rain fell in a downpour. The people were convinced the God of Heaven was looking out for His children.

It was now time for Roseberry to return to Sierra Leone and bring his wife to the new home prepared for her. He decided to go by train to the coast and go by steamer south to Freetown since the overland trail was arduous and time consuming.

On arriving at Conakry, Roseberry learned the next passenger boat to Freetown would not leave for two weeks. Never one to waste time, Roseberry looked for a coastal fishing boat that would take him. It was sixty miles south to Freetown on the Atlantic Ocean. The fisherman said he would take him for ten dollars.

On board, Roseberry couldn't move around because the boat was small and the quarters so limited. They set sail in the evening, but soon there was a calm that caused them to bob around on the swells that prevail along the coast. The next day brought a gentle breeze that developed into a strong gale. As they drove before the wind, the ropes holding the single mast broke, sending the sail into the sea. The mast was put into place and secured again. There was no light for night sailing but there was a compass on board and a quick check of the compass was dependent on the flare of an occasional match.

The journey usually made in a day stretched into the second. They could see the Freetown lighthouse, but again an offshore storm began to brew. The sail was lowered and the anchor cast since the water was more shallow. The anchor was a stone lashed to a forked stick and tied to a rope. It did not inspire confidence.

Since there was no shelter, Roseberry was given a piece of tarpaulin to put over himself. He committed himself to the Lord, then let the rolling of the boat put him to sleep. The storm was not severe and the boatmen assured him it was because there was a servant of God on board.

The third day at sea brought another period of calm. As was their practice, the boatmen took out their cow horns, blowing them loudly to call the breezes. The sound of horns soon grew louder as other stranded fishermen joined them. They baked in the hot tropical sun, but as evening came, a breeze set in, blowing toward shore. They were finally able to land after dark. It was an experience Roseberry would never forget.

Returning later with his wife, Roseberry was able to book deck passage on a Northbound Belgian steamer from Freetown. At Conakry, they boarded a train for the two-day ride inland. The narrow-gauge rails caused constant jolting, while the wood-burning steam locomotive sent a stream of sparks through the open windows. It was a relief to descend at Baro Station and settle in the primitive hut they now called home.

Roseberry and Ryan decided to build a boat because they were anxious to further the good news to the Soudan. They bought three boats being offered by the government to the highest bidder for thirteen dollars. The wooden boats had been used for transportation during the Great War and were dried out and unseaworthy, because they had been left on the river bank in the hot tropical sun.

The men picked out the best boat and began to caulk it. Unfortunately the new caulking also cracked and when the boat was launched, it filled with water and settled to the bottom of the river.

The men learned that tar or native shea butter must be mixed with the pitch in order for it to remain water proof. Finally, after much perseverance, the fifteen by three-foot boat equipped with an outboard motor was in the water and ready to go.

Roseberry and Lewis Ryan got a motley crew and provisions for the trip and set off downstream on the Niger River, one of the few great rivers of the world that flows in a northerly direction over much of its length. They were headed for Bamako, some four hundred and fifty miles away.

"The crew will bear description," Roseberry said. "The first man (our man of letters) was taken because he knew a little French. He said on starting that he had never carried loads on his head before. That troubled him, since loads had to be carried ashore when visiting towns.

"The cook claimed he was experienced in cooking—that he had in fact, cooked for a French officer. The first chicken he served was nicely browned. Nothing was wasted, because he cooked head, feet and all other parts! He always seemed happy and promised not to do it again. But when he also dried our tableware on his flowing gown, we decided to change cooks in order to preserve our appetites.

"People gathered together to hear the gospel message at nearly one hundred towns, some of them very large, that lay on our route. Returning soldiers spread the news of America's help in winning the

Great War and paved our way for a warmer welcome. People gave us chickens, eggs and milk for which we gave them a cash present.

"Lowlands along the river were marshy and we had to wade ashore, the water sometimes reaching to our waists. After a few days, one of our oars broke and we had to borrow tools to make a new one. The next calamity occurred at the Soudan boundary. The helper broke our only lantern, leaving us in darkness. We decided to schedule longer days so we could reach Bamako sooner. We found a lamp in town, but didn't buy it because it gave off more smoke than light."

After eighteen days, the men reached Bamako where they preached to large crowds in the open air every night. Desert men with long curly hair and flowing indigo gowns gathered around and heard the gospel for the first time. Other tribes were represented also. One man gave them a franc to show his appreciation. The missionaries met with the local official to get their passports signed and report on the reason for the trip.

"We reached about five thousand souls with the gospel on the trip and extended our mission," Roseberry said. "We are only beginning to realize the magnitude of this open door and the boundless opportunity we have."

After preaching for several nights in Bamako, Roseberry and Ryan began to prepare for the trip home. They arranged to have their boat tied alongside the government tugboat for half the trip, because the cost of gas for the outboard motor was excessively high. Covered with a tarpaulin to keep out the rain, the men tried to sleep the time away in camp cots atop their trunks. At the fork of the river they parted company with the tugboat, started their own motor and were soon home.

Alliance missionaries had at long last reached the French Soudan, only six days travel time from Timbuctoo. Light was coming to the Niger Valley and the dawn of the day spoken of so long ago by the prophet was about to shine, *"The people walking in darkness have seen a great light; on those living in the land of the shadow of death a light has dawned"* (Isaiah 9:2 NIV).

Chapter 10

GROWING PAINS

By 1922 it became obvious to the mission and its leaders in New York that if they were to occupy this vast new territory, a headquarters station was a necessity. Kankan, a few miles southeast of Baro was the likely choice. Bordered by the Milo River, a tributary of the Niger River, it was also the end of the rail line that connected the interior with the coast. Its well organized Colonial government assured its peace and tranquility and the streets were beautiful shaded drives. It was the hub of the developing Colony of French Guinea—a center for commerce, medical assistance and education.

A nice property just between the commercial sector and the residential areas of the population was soon obtained. A European style house was on the property. With some needed alteration it would provide living quarters as well as space for offices. Through the years, as funds came in, other buildings were put up. Eventually there was a two-story dwelling, chairman's bungalow, a print shop, a chapel, a garage to service mission vehicles and rooms to care for conference activities.

Soon we realized the need for motorized transportation. It was during the early twenties that the Ford Model T revolutionized travel. At the same time, the French government had developed a system of improved roads with bridges and river ferries. It was decided to purchase a Model T, which was the first of a fleet of cars God provided to hasten the spread of the gospel across the plains and through the forests of French West Africa.

Our first Model T had a Ford touring chassis with a bus body. It could carry many people and their baggage, but the springs were too weak and the motor too underpowered to haul the weight. The Ryan brothers were sent to build an advance station at Sikasso. Making their way eastward along the hilly road to that important center, they found out the deficiencies of the Model T the hard way.

When they came to a steep part of the road, the power failed. Many times they had to unload cement and building supplies, have it carried to the top of the hill, then reload—only to go a few miles and repeat the process!

Ah, yes, that wonder of wonders—the Model T! It was prone to leave one stranded time and time again. At night, the lights would suddenly go out. If the load was too heavy or the road too rough, the axle would break. And there were times when the engine would catch on fire and send passengers over the open sides until the flames were extinguished.

Getting it started was another thing. It could

easily wear out two or three men as they took turns cranking it to life. However, it was the pioneers' companion that helped open West Africa—a marvel in that era and place of primitive equipment. Without it, many goals might have been delayed considerably or not achieved at all.

In the northern region of French Guinea, rising from the coastal plain that bordered the Atlantic Ocean, is the Djallon Mountains. It was along those steep and twisting mountain roads that the Model T faced its greatest challenge.

In 1923 it was decided to seek sites for mission stations in addition to the one for the children's school at Mamou in that favorable climate. Labe, which was many miles further north, seemed to be an ideal location to begin an outreach of the Gospel to the Foulbe people who were proud and staunchly Muslim. Rev. and Mrs. Harry Watkins spent their careers there and were joined by Rev. and Mrs. John Johanson for a time.

The one road through these mountains was winding and narrow. Cars barely had room to pass. On these roads one faced mostly trucks whose drivers didn't slow for curves or seem to worry about weak or non-existent brakes. They were overloaded with commercial products topped high with passengers which made any trip hazardous.

Travel at night was out of the question since many trucks had no lights or at best, had only a kerosene lantern hanging near the window. In

59

addition, the Model T had its lapses, sometimes leaving its passengers grounded for hours along the road. However, without it, there could not have been the advance history records.

Dalaba was at a higher elevation about thirty miles from Mamou. A property was bought on the side of a hill overlooking a beautiful valley. It was a delightful spot for rest and recreation. Early morning mists filled the vale giving the illusion of a lake, hence the meaning of Dalaba, "Great Lake."

Terraces were excavated out of the hillside and several adobe thatch-roofed huts, resembling overgrown beehives after the style of the Foulbe people, were built. A big, rambling house was erected on the first level with a roof of corrugated iron to assure the deed to the property. Water was piped into a cistern from a nearby mountain spring.

The cooler climate was a refreshing change to weary missionaries and daily visits from venders of fruit, eggs and milk gave them a welcome change in diet. A whole month of such change, along with fun, fellowship and spiritual blessings at Dalaba sent these workers back refreshed and renewed. Roseberry was always concerned about the well-being of his staff. He used these times at Dalaba to get to know them better and encourage them. He knew that the renewal in spirit and body was necessary if they were to be able to face the debilitating climate and constant spiritual warfare back in their districts. In his heart, he walked the trails with them.

Chapter 11

THERE WERE GIANTS IN THE LAND

The advance into French West Africa was not without difficulty for the small band of missionary recruits. The adjustments to the culture of the people and the restrictions of a less than favorable government loomed as formidable "giants" to be overcome.

Language was also a barrier. Early missionaries had not learned French and had to speak to officials through an interpreter. Suspicious officials often made their work difficult by endless red tape and regulations and traveling in the district always had to be dutifully reported.

At one time, missionaries were required to deposit their return passage money on their entry into the country, thus tying up huge sums of money. A request to the Governor General at Dakar to accept a bond on mission property was backed by much prayer. The request was accepted.

Delay in acquiring land for mission stations became a major hindrance to advancement. Papers were pigeonholed for months. Then God provided a friend to meet this need. A Protestant lawyer in Dakar gave the mission much help. He wrote out the Articles of Incorporation for the Christian and Missionary Alliance and helped get the property matters settled.

The vastness of the land with its countless villages, tribes and languages proved to be a giant of tremendous proportions and the staff of pioneers was small. The French Guinea alone could have absorbed all the staff for years. The vision took them as far as Timbuctoo. After the first stage of establishing strategic centers was achieved, there had to be a time of intensive evangelism in which the first converts were gathered and trained. The final stage, establishing churches and the development of the National Church, would come later.

Early in the work, the mission had to face the fact that their forces were overdrawn to the the point that they could not cope with the situation. It was increasingly evident after World War II that the former colonies of French West Africa were moving toward becoming Independent Sovereign States.

Against that reality, Roseberry saw his staff too small to reach the vast unevangelized areas that still remained. He was a prime mover in the action of willingly turning over former Christian and Missionary Alliance fields to other evangelical missions. His goal of evangelizing all the peoples of

French West Africa superseded any feeling of possessiveness regarding territory to which the Christian and Missionary Alliance had laid claim.

The process began with The Conservative Baptist Foreign Missionary Society in 1947. They were given responsibility for several dialect areas of the Senoufo tribe in the Ivory Coast and were helped in getting property and other official business until they were established.

In 1949 Roseberry arranged for the well-known African language expert, Dr. William Welmers, to conduct language analysis consultations in various Senoufo dialects. This was of tremendous help to newly arrived Conservative Baptist Foreign Missionary Society missionaries in the Ivory Coast as well as to the Herbers struggling with Supyire in Sikasso.

Then the Evangelical Baptist Mission was given charge of Northern areas of what is now Mali. Among the centers where the Alliance had established stations earlier were the fanatically Muslim towns of Timbuctoo and Gao. The Koroboro, Songhoi, Tamasheck and Berber tribes, all nearly one hundred per cent Muslim, became their responsibility.

In 1954 the United World Mission was looking for territory in the Soudan to occupy for Christ. Dr. Sidney Correll, who was sponsored by the Christian and Missionary Alliance as a member of the West Africa Federation of Churches and Missions, contacted Roseberry. What is now Western Mali was offered to them.

Dr. Sidney Correll, Jr. M.D., in consultation with Dr. Vernier, a protestant surgeon and Head of Medical Services of the Soudan, was impressed with the great physical needs of peoples in the Senegal and other river plains and valleys where "river blindness" and "sleeping sickness" were pervasive.

It was mutually agreed that Dr. Correll make a survey of the area to discover the most advantageous center in which to establish a hospital and clinic. Roseberry asked Ralph, his son-in-law, to chauffeur Dr. Correll and act as his interpreter. The town of Kenieba was pinpointed as a strategic center for beginning their work. Malinke, Fulani, Khasonke and other tribes of the area had a large Islamic population.

God's strategy for confronting the "giants" was to be forwarded by evangelical missions and churches joining forces and collaborating together. Cooperation had been cordial with the Gospel Missionary Union from the earliest days. Missionary George Reed established its presence in the capital city of Bamako in 1921. The alliance assigned missionary personnel to assist Mr. Reed. The most significant teamwork between the missions was in the translation of the Scriptures into Bambara, the trade language. They proudly presented the entire Bible to the church during a

64

joint conference in 1964—a mighty "giant slayer" indeed was placed in their hands that day!

One by one the giants were overcome. New recruits were sent to France to become well prepared in the French language—a must for serving in a French territory. Tribal languages were analyzed and learned and Scripture translations begun. Chapels were built in cities and in remote villages. As men and women heard the call for service, vernacular Bible schools were opened to prepare pastors and teachers in various locations.

"By retrenching and drawing in our forces," Roseberry said, "we were able to develop the church. We pressed the work in two new pagan areas, raising a barrier against encroaching Islam. The Red Bobo country which was centered around Senekui in Soudan and Samogo country which was centered around Sourou in Upper Volta were staffed. The cliff dwelling Dogon tribe in northeast Soudan was opened and the Gospel was met with good response.

"By 1929 missionaries were sent to the Ivory Coast. They found many of the Baouli people's hearts already prepared by the preaching of a man named William Wade Harris. He was known by thousands as the 'black prophet.' He was a Liberian who, after experiencing the new birth, felt called to preach the gospel in the Gold and Ivory Coasts."

As West African tribes opened to the gospel, the head of another "giant" loomed on the horizon—

illiteracy. There were some twenty-five languages spoken across the vast territory, none of which had been reduced to writing. In an era when the science of linguistics had not yet been developed, missionaries had few scientific tools to work with, but these pioneers attacked this giant with a will and much prayer.

They attacked him by setting themselves to the development and production of primers that give a basic knowledge of reading, but also a knowledge of God and His plan of salvation. From primers, eager learners went on to the simple stories of the Bible and then the gospels that had been translated by that time. Short term Bible schools were held during slack times of the year, but the basic need for a full time Bible school was evident.

Even though the government ruled that all instruction should be in the French language, officials did not enforce the ruling. Bible schools were opened in strategic areas to train men and women in the Word using a language they could understand and communicate to their people.

The language question with the government was better resolved by 1942 with the help of two men sent by the Paris Evangelical Mission—Mr. Jean Keller and Mr. Georges Mabille. They argued the cause for teaching in the vernacular before officials and obtained favorable results. Mr. Mabille also helped the mission set up schools for children in French. These children were soon able to read all available literature. Many of these children became Christian school teachers and leaders, who in turn influenced others. The vision was becoming a reality!

Chapter 12

CAN A MUSLIM FIND CHRIST?

The little family with their few belongings tied in bundles carried on their heads started out by foot for the eighty-five mile walk from their village to Kankan, Guinea to see the field chairman. Ten francs and a bundle of rice was all they had. But Sayon the father, dressed in rags and partially blind, had an intense desire to serve the Lord in some way.

Blind Sayon, as he was known, had learned the hard way it is best to serve the Lord Jesus. His boyhood was like that of other boys. Before he was born, his parents had been obliged to flee before the blood-thirsty warriors of the Muslim conqueror Samory, who thought nothing of obliterating entire villages if they didn't submit and embrace Islam.

Being the youngest child of a large family, it was Sayon's job to chase the birds from the fields of ripening grain or cut firewood for his mother. Fortunately, when schools were opened by the French Colonial government, he was accepted and enrolled.

Later he was trained to be a carpenter and worked as a bridge builder and repairman of ferries on the rivers. The missionaries Clare and Ruth Ellenberger came to his town, built a chapel and preached the good news of Jesus Christ daily.

While making benches for the chapel, Sayon became convinced of the truth and accepted Christ as his Savior. Able to read the Word for himself, he made fast progress and was soon baptized. He became a witness in his home and at his work.

For three years Sayon walked with the Lord and was a source of encouragement. He worked as a carpenter for the government on a project to open a motor road. One day that road was blocked by a "sacred tree." The workers were paralyzed by fear. It was said that anyone who mutilated the tree would lose his leg.

Sayon stepped forward and said, "I'll cut off those branches. The God I serve will keep me from the power of the evil spirits." The tree was cut down and Sayon suffered no ill effects.

The flesh was weak, however, and yielding to Muslim intrigue, Sayon succumbed to the temptation to take a second wife. The Muslim religion allows up to four wives and the more wives one has, the greater the prestige. In taking another wife, Sayon broke his covenant with God and the light went out of his life. He soon stopped going to church. He was seemingly a prosperous man for a time, then his health began to fail. One day, after

Timbuctoo! Goal reached 1924. Roseberry standing in front of the memorial plaque to Major Laing, early British explorer slain by a hostile tribe in 1827.

A Model T Ford facilitates travel for early missionaries across vast areas of West Africa.

Evangelist Bokari Saba stands by a Model T, a vital help to evangelistic teams for reaching villages in Guinea forests.

A houseboat, *The Greg,* furnishes transportation on the Niger River.

The Ner-a-car served as transportation for Roseberry until a Model T was available.

The Roseberry family returns to Kankan for their fourth term in Africa, 1929.

Mission Headquarters at Kankan, "home" to the Roseberrys for many years.

eight days of intense headaches, his vision blurred so much that he couldn't continue his carpentry. He was obliged to move to the gold fields near the city of Siguiri to support his family.

Gold mining in Africa at that time was difficult and dangerous. Although he dug five or six shafts, Sayon found no gold. Soon, too ill to work, he had to remain in their hut and be supported by his faithful wife and two children.

One night, Sayon was in intense agony and after being told by people that he was going to die, he dreamed that the Lord stood by him.

"Sayon, you have left the Way," the Lord said. *"Return to Me and you will not die."*

On awakening, he was healed and his sight was partially restored! He arose from his cot and went with his family to the nearest town where there was a church. On Christmas Eve Christ was born anew in the prodigal's heart.

As the ragged little group entered the mission yard at Kankan, Clare Ellenberger was there to receive them. Several days later, Roseberry arrived from a tour and was overjoyed to hear the news of Sayon's repentance and return to the Lord. He was glad to place Sayon in the Kankan district, where he would faithfully minister for many years. Yes, a Muslim can find Christ!

Kankan, the second largest city in Guinea, West Africa, was an important trade center. Linked to the coast by a narrow-gauge railroad and to the hinterland by the Niger River, it seemed the ideal spot to locate the mission headquarters. The missionaries soon found Islam was predominant, even though there were pagan tribespeople in the city.

I remember as a child I was fascinated by the sight of throngs of large-robed people who congregated each day to pray at the big mosque located across from the mission property. We not only saw, but we could hear the murmur of their prayers to Allah. We were wakened each morning long before dawn by the stentorian voice of the prayer-caller. Five times a day, he reminded the "faithful" of their duty to pray.

At first crowds came to hear the missionaries preach.

"We began proclaiming the gospel in the city, section by section," Roseberry said. "Each evening we went to a new section and set up a small portable organ and opened the meeting. Soon the people realized our teaching differed from Islam in regard to the deity of Christ. They revered Jesus only as a prophet. 'God could not have a Son,' was their objection. One by one they would leave, never to return."

"You will never win a Maninka Muslim," a friend once told Roseberry.

A prominent Muslim teacher who resided in the city, was called a prophet. People came from far and wide to receive his blessing, bringing with them presents of cola nuts, money, women, camels, ostriches, cattle and sheep. He was considered a holy man who mysteriously went to the Muslim Holy City of Mecca every Friday and returned. His followers supposedly gained merit just by shaking hands with him.

It was in this hostile environment that Sayon remained a faithful witness to those about him. One of his spiritual children was Djansibouri, a prayer-caller at the local mosque in the town where Sayon served. A devoted Maninka Muslim, he had weighed the gospel against the Muslim religion and decided the gospel carried more weight. Some time after his conversion, he released his son, Timothy, to go to the Telekoro Bible School in the forest country. Timothy later served on the Bible school staff.

The Lord opened another ministry to Timothy later when he was asked to prepare messages in Maninka to be broadcast over radio station ELWA, a ministry in Monrovia, Liberia. Timothy was "The Voice of the Gospel" on a program that was received on transistor radios in homes throughout Guinea, reaching people that otherwise would not hear the truth. Pastor Timothy Conde is now pastoring the church at Faranah where he has started a Christian kindergarten and primary school.

Sayon would preach to the people going to the mosque for prayers at four-thirty in the morning. Some never made it there, but stopped to hear the message. This so irked the Muslim leaders that when the news of Sayon's death in 1981 was made known, there was rejoicing and dancing.

"He who troubled us is gone!" they said. Sayon was like a thorn in their side.

"Can Muslims be won for Christ?" Roseberry asked. "Yes, they can be—by the working of the Spirit of God in answer to prayer. This victory hinged on a small margin. A man who had failed was given another chance. Ragged, partly blind and poor, he did not look too prepossessing when I told him to go labor for the Lord in the district. He went and the victory was won!"

Chapter 13

THE WINNING TEAM

The glamour of missionary life may carry one along for a while, but the day comes when the soul faces reality. Roseberry often faced the tempter's query, *"Is it worth while? Were you really called to be a missionary?"*

"Once, early in my career I was traveling through a wilderness with my baggage carriers and had injured my finger," he said. "It was a small scratch and I thought it would soon heal. Before long, however, the scratch became painful and red lines ran up my arm. Blood poisoning! I knew the symptoms. I reached toward heaven and claimed deliverance.

"By evening I felt very ill. The road by bicycle had been rough and the sun hot! I preached to the people as was my custom, but, as I went to bed, I felt very feverish.

"My hut for the night was poorly kept. Rats ran up one side of the mosquito net and around the poles in the ceiling and roof. The fever raged on and I longed for companionship, but the Lord's presence was very real to me and I felt better in the morning.

I was able to ride to the railway and take a train home."

Jesus' message, *"Lo, I am with you always . . ."* was true—Jesus had been Roseberry's companion. Blessing often comes out of great trial.

Promptness was a real part of Roseberry's character. He was often called "Mr. Yesterday" by colleagues, since he was usually ahead of his schedule.

"The time came for an important committee meeting at Bamako, the capital of the Soudan," Roseberry said. "Mr. Michael Kurlak, my vice-chairman, and I had a long road to travel and it was the rainy season. Heavy trucks had cut deep ruts in the road and there was no way to get around them. It was too slippery to ride on top of the ruts and a swamp was on either side.

"We soon bogged down and I had to put brush and timber under the wheels to pry the car out of the muck. This was accomplished once, but the second time the car really stuck. After building a piece of road with stones and sticks, we tried to cross, but the car skidded into the mud again and the heat began to sap our strength and resolve. A messenger was sent for help. Soon, about twenty men came, and by tying a chain to the front of the car, they literally dragged the car to higher ground.

"Evening came, but the lights wouldn't work and we had to camp by the wayside for the night. Bed and bath were impossible and the evening meal was scanty, but we could feel the Lord's presence.

"I had never been late to a meeting, but we arrived at our destination a half-day late. When we met the following day, the Lord was there and the Spirit ministered in every meeting. It was a touch of revival. We learned a great lesson in that meeting. Having the Spirit of God in control of our lives was of utmost importance. One of the greatest difficulties of the Christian experience is to **wait on Him until He speaks**. We must have the spirit to guide us!"

Roseberry remembered a sermon Dr. Simpson preached in the spring of 1909. His text was, *"The fear of the Lord is wisdom and to depart from evil is understanding"* (Job 28:28). It was a clarion call for victorious living in the face of the enemy.

The Holy Spirit was Roseberry's constant companion and guide throughout his life. He had learned the only way to travel the highway of holiness was to rise early each day and pray and meditate on the Word of God.

As their only child, I remember awakening to the noise of the mechanical kerosene lantern being wound long before daybreak and I knew my parents were meeting God. They were on the winning team!

Chapter 14

THE HOUR OF POWER

On any given day, the "chug-chug" of a moped would break the serenity of the headquarters station at Kankan. The printers were busy running their machines in the print shop. The chairman and his staff were engaged with mission business at their desks. But all came to a stop as the uniformed man stepped up to the door. The faded blue folded paper in his hand meant only one thing—news from far away!

However, many times it contained tragic news. I remember many of these telegrams that brought overwhelming sorrow. Their often cryptic lines told of the death of little children of the missionary family. Beautiful twin boys of Ethyl and George Bell died from an overdose of a malaria drug. Paul and Mable Freligh laid their little Mary in a solitary grave on a Guinea hillside due to measles and pneumonia and absence of medical care. Mary Stamm, infant daughter of Charles and Sadie Stamm, was a victim of a hostile Soudan climate. And the little son of Esther and Andrew Hyndman, the Clifford Ryan baby and others also suffered untimely deaths. Usually the loved ones would bear their suffering alone. The long distances involved made traveling out of the question. However, comfort came as the missionary family held the faded blue sheet of paper before the Lord and prayed.

Prayer was the power tool of the early missionaries entering the French Soudan. Annual conferences began with days of fasting and prayer. Prayer assumed a preeminent place in all meetings. Before opening evangelistic meetings in a new area, the staff spent two days in prayer and fasting. Is it any wonder that by the 1930's, towns and villages were responding to the gospel and key men and women were receiving special anointings of the Spirit to evangelize their people?

During the days of Roseberry's leadership intercessory prayer was a way of life. Every day at four p.m. the missionaries on each station met for prayer. It became an hour of power.

Was the mission trying to get properties or was permission to build tied up by government red tape? Were funds low in the coffer and hindering advancement? Was a co-worker going through illness and suffering? Answers came again and again as the missionaries prayed and God was glorified.

Perhaps one of the most frequent and important requests that came was for rain on the land. A good example is the opening of work in the Dogon tribe. In June of 1931, the Francis McKinneys had taken up residence in Sangha, which is located on the edge of the Sahara Desert. The Dogon people were cliff dwellers and fanatical fetish worshippers, even known to practice ritualistic cannibalism. The McKinneys arrived during a time of great crisis. Rain had not fallen and the crops were drying up. All efforts to invoke their gods had failed. The Dogon village elders were desperate.

The chief and seven old men approached the missionaries and said, "We have done all we can to get rain and have failed. You have been telling us that when you pray to your God in Jesus' name, he hears and answers your prayers."

The McKinneys told the story of Elijah—how the three-year drought was broken by prayer. The villagers were urged to repent of their sins and believe in the true God of heaven.

"Oh," replied the chief, "if God will answer your prayer and send rain to save our crops, we will repent and believe in Him."

Crisis time! The missionaries at Sangha went down on their knees, leaving their food untouched. Three hours went by. Suddenly a clear sky turned dark and thunder rumbled. The dark clouds opened and rain fell on the parched ground. God's power was shown in an unforgettable way!

Seventeen men prayed to God for forgiveness of sin in Jesus name that day. Among them was Assegarema the Blacksmith who became a true spiritual leader in the church through the years.

Chapter 15

ANGEL OF MERCY

On any day of the week a motley crowd of sad people could be found sitting at my mother's back door, waiting for Madame's tender loving care. Children with puss-filled infected eyes, open inflamed sores, raw untended burns and feverish babies—all found relief there. (Madame was the name given Edith Roseberry by the missionary staff and Africans who soon found out where to come in time of need).

An African trucker with a badly burned arm appeared one Sunday. After carefully applying a healing balm, Madame bandaged the arm and told him to go to the city clinic Monday.

On Monday he was back. When asked why he didn't go to the city clinic, he replied, "Oh Madame, your medicine is better! I am coming to you!"

She could not turn him away, but treated him day after day until the arm was healed. He went away with no word of thanks.

Many months later, as Roseberry was traveling along a forest road, he met a truck on a curve. When he tried to evade the truck, his car slid into a ravine and finally anchored on the stump of a tree.

They were miles from any source of help, but as they mused and prayed, another truck came along and stopped. The African chauffeur was a man of action. He looked over the situation, tied a sapling to the car with rope and vines from the forest, and soon the truck tugged the car up the 45 degree grade to the road. When Roseberry offered to pay him, the chauffeur replied, "You need pay me nothing. Did not your old woman treat my arm when it was burned?"

Madame's tender loving care had not been forgotten! (In African culture "old woman" is a term of respect).

As the chairman's wife, Edith Roseberry often traveled with her husband as he visited mission stations over the vast expanse of French West Africa. Many times she ministered to the missionaries. While she and Roseberry were visiting the George Powells in the Ivory Coast, their small son, Archie, got very ill. Edith took him in her arms and walked the floor, calling upon the Lord. He was delivered almost immediately.

Another time, Philby Stoddard was weak from dysentery and could not have stood much more. Again, taking the little one in her arms, Edith prayed until relief came.

"We appreciated your ministry, but you are what you are because of Madame," missionaries later told Roseberry.

Roseberry appreciated the role his wife played in his ministry. While he was away from home for weeks at a time on administrative duties, she would calmly meet emergencies that arose. She knew how to be discrete whenever she knew of problems in the missionary family and was not given to gossip.

"No hour was too late that she would not arise from her bed and welcome a weary traveler and show him a room," Roseberry added, "Every room had been carefully cleaned, water furnished and clean towels were on the rack. She was that type of woman. She was the mother of the mission for many years."

Edith's heart reached out to the women and girls of Africa. She yearned that they might have the appreciation and cooperation of their husbands. She could identify with their wrongs and sorrows. Their long hours in the fields and household chores, providing constant care of children did not go unnoticed.

"I can only say the Lord gave me a helpmeet that stood by me through the trying years when we were up against many problems," Roseberry said.

(Edith Roseberry told her own story in the booklet, *"From Kansas Prairies to African Forests*, copyright 1957).

Chapter 16

HELPING HANDS

As World War II reached into North Africa, missionary work became more and more complicated. The staff dwindled to a mere thirty missionaries. It was not difficult to leave the country, but it became almost impossible to re-enter. There was a hostile government to placate. How would they survive? God had a plan!

Help came in the form of a Frenchman from the Paris Evangelical Mission, Pasteur Keller, a former missionary in Equatorial Africa. He was sent to represent the mission to the Governor General in Dakar. The governor's signature on Roseberry's papers saved embarrassing questions in 1942 when he crossed the border on his return to French Guinea.

Monsieur Mabille later joined Monsieur Keller and both men rendered valuable service to the mission. When the American army invaded North Africa, most missionaries were interned at their stations. When Monsieur Keller found out, he was able to have them released. During a time when Americans were under utmost suspicion and the work of evangelism was considered worthless, these men were a great asset.

"The war had brought difficulties that made it necessary for Protestant missions to organize a Federation of Missions in 1945 and a preliminary council was formed," said Roseberry. "The council was later formally organized with the approval of the Colonial Government. Monsieur Mabille and Pasteur Keller played a vital role as General Secretary of the Federation.

"Based at Dakar, the seat of the French government in West Africa, the men were able to look after the affairs that concerned the missions. Our relation to the government and the attitude toward us soon began to look different. When the charter was drawn up, a number of new missions were able to enter the territory, opening up new areas to the gospel.

"The obtaining of entry and residence visas was speeded up, concessions were granted and sites for schools in good localities for minimum prices were obtained," Roseberry continued. "Through their efforts, our bush schools and Bible schools were put on a sound basis. When demands from Christian parents for their children's education in the official language of French could not be denied, French Primary Schools were started. One important issue was our school for missionaries' children at Mamou. Since schools that taught in English were not permitted, it was only after many years that our school was given legal status."

In 1948 one situation during the opening of an outstation in the Sikasso District in the Soudan could have been serious.

"Ralph Herber and his wife did a lot of traveling meeting the people and preaching the gospel in the villages," Roseberry explained. "In the meantime, they were digging holes to plant fruit trees at the Farakala station. A state police trooper reported to the governor at Dakar that Herber was prospecting for diamonds for the American government. Mr. Keller was faced with the accusation before the governor. 'What's this all about?' he asked. Keller dismissed it with a laugh saying, 'That's the mentality of a Gendarme for you.'"

Had it not been for his intervention, a missionary career could have suddenly ended.

Never one to be limited by circumstances, Roseberry moved forward on all fronts. When the U.S. Government made provision for him to return to Africa in July of 1942, there was a need for a Bible Training Center in the Ivory Coast. The mission staff was decimated because of the travel conditions during World War II and Roseberry felt he should offer to supervise the building of the school himself.

A fine property had been found in the town of Bouake, a large city in the center of the country. Though Rev. and Mrs. George Powell, pioneer missionaries in the Ivory Coast, had a training program going, it was felt that a larger center was needed on the out-skirts of town. The old property had to be sold in order to develop the new lot granted by the government.

"One morning I had a strong impression an offer would be made that day," Roseberry said. "Not long after sunrise, I saw a man coming on a bicycle. This man made us an offer of 800,000 francs ($16,000). We soon closed the deal and a big carton of French francs was sent over. We worked for two nights 'til near midnight, counting the currency to get them ready for the bank. Imagine, $16,000 worth of francs—and much of it in small bills, some tattered and torn and very filthy.

"We wasted no time," he added. "We ordered brick from a nearby kiln, purchased lumber at the mill and hired a mason. Grass had to be cleared with a native bush knife, because no bulldozer was available. Rocks for the foundations were excavated right on the site."

Help was needed once again. Andrew Dupont, the superintendent of one of the saw mills in the Ivory Coast forest and a representative of a big firm in France was valued for his keen business ability.

"Mr. Dupont and his small son, Peter, visited me and asked if he could be any help," said Roseberry. "He saw that I was pressed and alone in the work. I felt led to say yes and I was not disappointed.

"For a while Mr. Dupont worked as an associate missionary. He was generous with his time and money. When he saw a need for printing Bible portions, he gave money for a printing press. Later he gave funds for a car. His wife had passed away earlier and when he married a school teacher from the French Mission, she proved a blessing also, because she was able to get the Bible school established in accordance with government regulations.

"After a time, the Duponts joined the French Mission and were sent to a town near the Liberian border. The people there had a reputation of being cannibals, but the Duponts' ministry was blessed and churches were established."

These efforts were not in vain. With God's blessing, Bouake became a center of the Alliance Mission in the Ivory Coast and from there, the Word has gone out far and near until scores of churches and tens of thousands of believers sing the praises of Christ the Lord throughout the land.

Chapter 17

A LOVE FOR THE CHILDREN

My father loved children and was a great story teller. I am told when he visited missionary homes he would put the little ones on his knees and tell them stories. He was not beyond high drama, for sometimes a small boy would suddenly find himself suspended in mid air by the seat of his pants!

He was always concerned about the health and well being of those children.

"In the early days, it was considered impossible to raise children on the field," he said. "The climate was hot and humid and there was no provision for their education. When we crossed the border into French Guinea, we looked for a site for a missionaries' children school. The Fouta Hills, whose highest point reaches nearly 4,000 feet above sea level, seemed ideal. We chose a site near Mamou close to the Conakry-Niger railway at an elevation of not quite 3,000 feet."

A remodeled hotel became a home away from home for the Missionary Kids in 1929.

I was a charter member of that school and can say it truly became that home away from home! Mr.

and Mrs. David Rupp, with the help of gifted teachers such as Miss Erma Sigler, provided the loving care and training.

"They were faithful in laying a spiritual foundation in each boy's and girl's life," Roseberry said.

Later a new school was constructed on a nearby hilltop where there was room for expansion with a beautiful view of the surrounding valleys and hills. Old Mamou "grads" still remember their explorations on Sugar Loaf Mountain, Castle Rock and Baboon Rock.

The school grew and later included the children of other missions. Big cisterns caught rain water and provided water sufficient enough even for a swimming pool. A plentiful supply of fruit and vegetables provided a good diet for the children.

"I feel that one of the most important ministries of my life has been helping in this vital work," said Roseberry. "We visited the school twice a year for evangelistic services and saw lives changed and dedicated to the Lord." Some of these MK's later returned as missionaries.

High school was not included in the program in the early years.

"My daughter had to take her high school course by correspondence with the American School from Chicago," Roseberry said. "On graduation in 1938, she was able to enter Taylor University in Upland, Indiana.

"The next step of faith was to send Ruth to college. We had about $120 saved, but her allowance ended when she was eighteen. However, she was able to get a $125 work scholarship. We still thank God that we were able to care for her expenses. In her second year we returned to the States for furlough and lived on Taylor campus. We had more opportunity to fully help with needed funds when the war prevented our return to Africa. It was a red-letter day to see our daughter receive her diploma.

"Ruth received her call to the mission field while working at Maranatha Bible Camp in Muskegon, Michigan in 1942. After her graduation from Taylor, she was offered a scholarship for further studies at Wheaton College, but she and her fiancé felt led to go to the Nyack Missionary Training Institute. My wife could not return to the field in 1942, so she kept house for Ruth until she and Ralph Herber were married in 1943.

"Ruth needed a wedding dress and it was provided in an unusual way," Roseberry said. "A missionary leafing through a book in the library of the mission rest home in Guinea discovered a large sum of money which had been placed there and forgotten. Since the owner was not known, the missionary family agreed that it be sent to Ruth for her wedding trousseau. The Lord is always on time and meets every trusting heart that will follow Him all the way."

Mamou School continued until it was closed by the pro-Marxist government of Sekou Toure in 1971 when Guinea drastically restricted almost all foreign missions operations. Fortunately, a good school was being conducted by the Conservative Baptist Mission in the Ivory Coast. They gladly received children from our Christian and Missionary Alliance fields in Africa. They had realized early that the policies of the new government would eventually make operating the Mamou School impossible. As a result, the Ivory Coast Academy was ready to receive the children and a smooth transition took place as once more, the Lord graciously provided.

Chapter 18

TRAVEL WEST AFRICAN STYLE

You couldn't be a missionary very long in West Africa before you knew the meaning of "WAWA," the slogan "West Africa Wins Again." It became a day by day reality which provided a humorous release from frustrations that often occurred when traveling. As field chairman, Roseberry had many experiences when he made frequent tours to encourage his staff of missionaries.

Roseberry received a model A Ford while on his third furlough. It was a welcome change from the old model T that had worn out its usefulness and he looked forward to setting out on his first trip to visit the stations. I remember vividly when he and Mr. Fermin Sauve, a newly arrived missionary recruit, climbed into the shiny black car and pulled out of the yard.

Much to our dismay, before very long, they limped back into the station. A grass fire had swept across the plain, burning out the log supports of a crude mud and stone bridge. The men had no inkling that what appeared to be a bridge was a mere mud and stone shell. Without warning, the Model A plunged down into the dry creek bed below and bounced to a stop on the other side.

Thankful that their lives were spared, they hobbled back home. Fermin Sauve injured his back. But the greatest tragedy to me, a five-year-old, was what happened to my father. He had lost his gold-crowned front teeth when his mouth hit the steering wheel. The new model A would need extensive repairs before they could try again.

"Quarantine for yellow fever often means closing main roads. A *sanitary passport* must be carried at all times and checked at every barrier," Roseberry said. "On one tour from Guinea into the Ivory Coast, we were stopped at a barrier near the city of Nao, one of the highest mountains in Guinea. We had to spend the night there and have our temperature taken by the health inspector in the morning before we were allowed to go on.

"After a pleasant ride through the forest we had to pass another barrier upon entering the Ivory Coast. Getting out of the car, we noticed gas running from the tank where it had been pierced by a stone. Gas was obtainable only in large centers and we risked being stranded in the wilderness. We had learned early the trick of stopping gasoline leaks by applying soft soap to the hole. This works fine, but of course soap must be replaced frequently when traveling through water. This barrier proved to be a blessing. We wouldn't have discovered our loss until it was too late."

Traveling with some of the missionary men into the Bocanda district of the Ivory Coast, it was necessary to take a boat down the river.

"I expressed my desire for some fresh fish for supper," Roseberry said. "A small fish was obtained and while waiting for supper, we took a bath in the only place available. A stockade from rough-hewn slabs of wood was built out in the town square. By using a small calabash (a scooped-out dry gourd), one could pour water over the body and be refreshed.

"The fish was not too tasty, but we ate it. I thought a fish bone had lodged in my throat when I felt a smarting sensation later. My throat became sore and inflamed.

"When our visit was over, we decided to walk back overland. Elephants had spoiled the road and made it difficult walking through the maze of their giant foot prints. We then resumed our tour of the field and entered the Soudan, which is now Mali. My throat worsened, so we thought it would be best to go to the capitol city of Bamako and see a specialist.

"After a rough ride over badly grooved roads that resembled a washboard, we arrived at the Gospel Missionary Union's Headquarters. We were met with the enthusiastic outcry 'Here is Roseberry!'

"We learned some newly arrived missionaries

needed my signature on a bank draft to secure funds necessary to get their car through customs and pay their bills. Once again God had used a seeming mishap to enable them to meet a need of which they were unaware. My throat began to improve as soon as we started toward Bamako. Before long it was back to normal."

The hazards of traveling African roads were many, especially during unseasonable tropical downpours. Every year vehicles plunged off slippery roads and turned over, mangling the passengers who rode precariously perched atop the load.

"We started early in the morning hoping to arrive in Bouake on the Ivory Coast by afternoon," Roseberry said, describing an experience in the Gold Coast. "The first part of the road was paved and we sped along at a good clip. At the end of the pavement, the road was like a quagmire in some places. Soon the clay became so deep we could not climb a small hill. We tried to push, but the car edged to the side of the road and was in danger of going into the ravine. We had no tools to dig the mud from under the wheels, so as the sun set, we scattered to collect leaves and brush to put under the wheels for traction. It was a dangerous thing to do, feeling around on the ground where snakes or scorpions might be lurking—particularly at night.

"Our fellow traveler, Gordon Timyan, found a cutlass left by the side of the road—an astonishing provision! With that, we were able to clear the mud and get traction enough to get up the hill. We were thankful for the Lord's deliverance because we were afraid that a truck would round the curve and plunge down on us. In fact, we hardly got to the top before a truck plunged into the gully."

Chapter 19

MUSA HAS COME

I could see the look of concern on my parents' faces as they opened the faded blue sealed paper. It had only a date, a place of origin and a simple sentence, *"Musa has come."* But it spoke volumes. Musa was the mission code name for that dreaded disease called yellow fever.

I was only eleven years old, but this sudden crisis of the young mission made an impact I never forgot.

Yellow fever is an acute, infectious and often fatal tropical disease caused by a virus transmitted by the bite of a mosquito known as the yellow fever mosquito. It is characterized by high fever, jaundice, vomiting and diarrhea. There was no vaccination in the 1930's. The only protection was to restrict the movement of the population and require people in an effected area to take shelter under mosquito nets from sun-up to sun-down.

In July of 1931 the already small staff of workers was suddenly decimated, leaving a baby without parents, two small children without a mother and a grieving husband without a wife.

"The epidemic of yellow fever began in the Ivory

Coast, sweeping northward to Bobo-Dioulasso, Upper Volta and to Sikasso in the French Soudan," Roseberry said. "At Bobo five officials died. When the disease was discovered, the Sikasso doctor refused to believe the reported diagnosis until it had claimed more victims and official word had come from the capitol."

Two missionary couples were stationed at Sikasso—the Fred Joders and the Rudolf Andersons. "Ella Joder became ill and her husband, Fred soon contracted the fever. Ethel Anderson cared for them, but she was soon taken ill herself." Roseberry continued, "Rudolf Anderson hurried home from an executive committee meeting at Kankan. He was delayed along the way when the front spring of the Model T Ford broke and parts were not readily available. He arrived at Sikasso to find his three comrades very ill.

"Mrs. Joder grew worse and passed away as Anderson was giving her a drink of water. He had been carrying on alone, night and day and was relieved when other missionaries came to help. Earnest Howard, George Powell, Helen Sherwood and Clara Klint put their own lives on the line as they cared lovingly for their co-workers. Once a person entered the city, they could not leave until the quarantine was lifted.

"Mr. Joder passed the crisis and was improving when Mrs. Anderson succumbed on July 15—Mr. Anderson passed away the following morning.

Neither were conscious at the end and neither knew that the other was taken. The governor of the colonies stood at the graveside himself and gave words of comfort saying, 'They came to help lift this country as I have done. Their lives have not been spent in vain. They rest with God.'"

The head medical officer made every white person leave the town at night and sleep in huts in the surrounding villages until the plague was over. After Rudolf's death, the house was sealed until Roseberry could come and take care of the estate. A hastily written will made out on Anderson's death bed named Roseberry the universal executor and guardian of his child. Later the United States courts wouldn't recognize the validity of the hastily written will, so Edward, known as Teddy, was committed to the care of his maternal grandmother who raised him.

Misrikoro, aptly named by Fred Joder as *"Misery's Corner,"* was two adobe huts with thatch roofs that stood beside the bush road going south of Sikasso toward the Ivory Coast border. The town itself was a center for Muslim study. The village name really meant *"beside the mosque,"* and was the home of a powerful Muslim teacher.

A large outcropping rock nearby contained several caverns and internal passageways which provided places for sacrifices and secret rites. It became a tourist attraction in later years. Dried bones of sacrificial animals still clutter the scene.

Stones are black from the blood of many offerings and white chicken feathers festoon a glob of fresh blood, marking a recent sacrifice.

During the yellow fever epidemic, our missionary colleagues occupied those two huts that were intended as a motel for travelers until the quarantine was lifted. We passed Misrikoro often during our years in the Sikasso district, because we repeatedly traveled that road.

The grass roofs gradually disintegrated and the walls became heaps of mud, but it was a constant reminder of those who were there before us and the sacrifice they made to take the gospel to the Senoufo tribe. It was a task they could not complete in their lifetime.

There were other crises faced by the West African staff and other lives were laid down, but they pushed on undaunted. Reports of victories won, men, women and children being born into the family of God would soon come.

"We cannot retreat," Roseberry said. "Volunteers have already come forward for Sikasso and the Senoufo people. Impere was the first convert from the Senoufo tribe. He was crippled by polio as a child and was called 'Three legged Impere,' because he used a long stick to help him walk. He hobbled out to the cemetery at the edge of town and bowed at the graves of his beloved teachers. After prayer, he encouraged a fellow believer with these words, 'Do not let this trouble weaken your faith.'"

The news of three promising missionaries' lives being laid down for the gospel's sake swept across the homeland. A great volume of prayer ascended to the Lord of the Harvest and renewed commitments to prayer and intercession were made across the Alliance constituency.

Jesus said, *"Unless a kernel of wheat falls to the ground and dies, it remains only a single seed. But if it dies, it produces many seeds"* (John 12:24 NIV).

Chapter 20

WEARY WARTIME TRAVELERS

By the fall of 1943 the war was raging in Europe and the Vichy government was losing ground in North Africa and other African colonies. Travel by ship was becoming possible again, but it was tedious. In September a band of some fifty missionaries from eight different mission boards were poised, ready to return to Africa. My mother, Edith Roseberry, was among those leaving. It had been fourteen months since her husband had returned to West Africa.

Soon after leaving the peaceful New York harbor, a storm struck the French liner. Waves as high as the second deck broke over the ship and port holes shattered, letting in the sea water to soak the cabins. Dishes fell out of cabinets and skidded across the floor. Steamer chairs slid across the deck as the ship pitched and rolled from side to side. The fifty missionaries on board prayed and claimed God's promises—the storm abated and calm was restored. Even the unsaved regarded it as Divine deliverance.

After some three weeks at sea, they were safely ashore in Lisbon, Portugal and the waiting began. They booked into a hotel and spent many hours enjoying the city's shops and beautiful parks. Not knowing the language of the people there, the missionaries soon became experts in the art of signing.

When a carbuncle developed on Edith's eye, she saw a Catholic doctor who treated her eye. Amazed at her rapid recovery from the serious eye infection, the doctor and his wife asked a lot of questions concerning her work and faith. They were interested to know the difference between her faith and the Catholic Religion, which gave her a chance to witness.

By November 15, the party was on a small cargo ship heading down the African coast. They stopped briefly at the Madeira Islands for a pleasant interlude.

"The port is beautiful. Cream colored houses reach to the top of high mountains, their red tile roofs contrasting with the green background of gardens and trees," said Edith.

Madeira Island is known for its beautiful embroidered linens. The traders were willing to trade for warm clothes, so the party took advantage of these offers because before long, they wouldn't need the warm clothing anyway!

Nearing the West Coast of Africa, the ship ran into troubled seas and lurched from side to side.

The cabins were uncomfortable as portholes had to remain closed. Just moments after Franklin Ballard had been thrown from his bed to the floor, a fan detached from the ceiling and landed on his pillow.

Bissau, the main port of Portuguese Guinea was a welcome sight. It was not "home," but it was on African soil. They had been in route for two months and it was a relief to everyone to be on land again.

"I am nearly fed up with fish," Edith said. "We have had fish twice a day since leaving the States. Boiled fish with boiled potatoes is not too tasty."

In December the little party of missionaries were nearing their final destination. Some of them were able to get passage on the Dakar-Bamako railway, but others had still another wait. Edith and Grace Patterson were able to get passage on an aircraft which saved them thirty-two hours of travel time.

Some of the party had to board a small coastal plane that landed on water. There was a high wind and the plane rolled from side to side as it taxied for take off.

"I looked across the aisle at Elroy Roffe and thought he was dying," Edith said. "I forgot my own troubles and began to plead the blood for his protection. Mrs. Roffe rubbed his cold, limp arms from across the aisle. Thankfully after the plane was airborne, Mr. Roffe felt better. Prayer always brought us through during such difficulties."

After four hours by plane from Dakar, Edith and her traveling companion, Grace Patterson, reached

Bamako, Soudan on Christmas day.

"What joy to think we are really here and well after three months of travel, trials and perplexities," she continued. "We ate our Christmas dinner at the hotel and enjoyed real vegetables."

On New Years Day of 1944, Edith and Robert were again working together as partners to meet the needs of the West African team. They would have many responsibilities in a time when supplies of every nature were extremely limited, but they would also have many opportunities to prove their God.

Chapter 21

THE MANY HATS OF A FIELD DIRECTOR

During high school, I secretly resented my lack of personal identity. In Africa I was the *chairman's daughter.* During furlough times I was always *Roseberry's daughter.* It was only during my college years that I escaped those labels because my parents were not known at Taylor or in the community.

The Mamou school for missionaries' children did not provide for high school in 1935. Therefore, I was living at home in Kankan, Guinea on the Mission Headquarters Station, taking grades ten through twelve by correspondence from the American School in Chicago, Illinois.

Memories flood my mind as I remember the early morning ritual in the room next to mine. Long before the sun rays would awaken me, I would hear the squeak of the mechanical kerosene lamp being wound up. A clockwork device supplied oxygen for the yellow flame that illuminated my parents' prayer time.

Once roused, I would often listen in. I could hear them praying for me, the lost peoples of Africa, the missionary staff and the problems faced in the enormous task of building the Church of Christ in a pagan society.

Hearing their prayers was a heavy responsibility for a teenager, knowing that some people might ask questions concerning matters which must be kept confidential. Now I understand that their prayer time was the secret behind the work that has culminated in a strong, growing church with Spirit-filled national leaders and a corps of Bible trained men and women.

Since I have become an adult, I have appreciated the responsibilities my father carried as Field Director for French West Africa. He considered the directorship an honor, but it was also a great responsibility. He soon found out he had to wear the hat of a diplomat.

"The responsibility was a heavy one which drove me to the Lord for an anointing, so that I could lead the army forward to victory," Roseberry said. "Starting with a small force of workers in 1919, the field staff numbered nearly 60 by 1928. They came to the field with youth, enthusiasm and ambition. Sometimes it was difficult fitting them all together."

A leader must be sensitive to the needs of his co-workers, especially during times of crisis. There were no hospitals or competent medical personnel in the early years. One night Ruth Ellenberger was near exhaustion delivering her first child. She was sustained as she heard Roseberry's strong voice lifted up in prayer in the next room of the mission house. He was there on his knees until the crisis passed and Paul Ellenberger was born.

Many times new missionaries could not cope with certain circumstances and they would be tempted to return home. On numerous occasions Roseberry would counsel with them in a spirit of love and help them find a new sphere of ministry to which they were better suited. Prayer was the key to his leadership. He prayed daily for his staff and their needs, calling them by name before the Lord.

Roseberry wore the hat of a motorcyclist during the early years when travel was a problem.

"The mission had only one car for years," Roseberry said. "This made it difficult to reach the stations or gather together for Annual Conference. There was no bus route or air service, so we did not meet very often, because we were separated by many miles. I used a *Ner-a-car* which was similar to a motorcycle with a side car. But it was not convenient, because I couldn't carry passengers or much baggage. We did use steamers on the Niger River and some available railroads when going North."

The picture greatly changed when roads were constructed and vehicles were obtained as the country developed.

Roseberry put on the hat of a builder/architect

early because construction became a real part of the first pioneers' work.

"Lumber was hard to find in the Soudan as there were few trees and they were too hard to cut," he said. "We had excellent men in the forests of Guinea who could handle any tree. We made a contract to take care of them on the job and pay them per yard on lumber, thus saving two-thirds of the cost. We learned something about the art of burning brick from my cousin who was superintendent of a brick works in Clearfield, Pennsylvania. By looking ahead in the building program, time and money was saved and by finding materials and stockpiling them, the process was speeded up."

When there was a need to build a new mission residence and Bible school classrooms at Bouake, Ivory Coast, Roseberry wore an architect/ construction hat. This was in a period after he returned during war years. His wife had not yet joined him and he worked with Walter Olsen to design houses that were compatible with the climate. For many years thereafter, their plan was copied in other building projects.

As the missionary family grew, health needs could not be ignored. One day after suffering the pain of a bad tooth, Roseberry decided to put on a dentist hat.

"When I came home on furlough, a dentist took me into his office and showed me many things," he

Pastor Marika Keita, first President of the National Church of the C. & M.A. in Mali, organized in 1960.

Roseberry is decorated with the Medal of the French Legion of Honor by the Governor of the Colonies. The Late Dr. A. C. Snead looks on. 1952.

Roseberry proudly wears the medal conferred on him which also honors his co-workers.

Typical Muslim Mosque constructed in a style found in the Soudan. Missionaries found such structures preceeded them into the interior of West Africa.

Kankan Gospel Chapel built by Roseberry in early 1950s.

Early baptismal scene in Dogon country. A pool from rain is a water source in a dry land.

Three evangelists, all converted Muslims: Bokari Saba, the Bozo fisherman; Mamadou Keita, the Mason from Gao; and Belko, a Foulani ex-soldier from the Mopti.

Roseberry and Cova Zoumanigue, early worker from the
Toma tribe, Macenta, Guinea.

Dogon elders in front of the adobe brick Chapel at Sangha,
Soudan, 1951.

said. "Other dentists helped and I obtained some dental instruments and was able to do a fair job. It was my custom to carry a hand-run dental outfit by which I could give first aid. When the Lord helped me to relieve the pain of an official who had an abscessed wisdom tooth, which had to be extracted, it created much good will. Once I asked the railroad station master for a favor. 'You go over and pick out what you want from the shop. You fixed my wife's teeth years ago,' he said."

After Mr. W. G. Lewis, a dentist from Nebraska, came to visit Africa, he went home with a desire to help train missionaries in dentistry. He trained two missionary nurses, Prudence Gerber and Dorothy Adam and gave them the equipment they needed.

"What a blessing that has been to our missionaries and their children at school," Roseberry said.

Perhaps his greatest challenge as field director was to discern and choose men who would feel the call to reach their people for Christ and have the spiritual gifts to do it. Bokari Saba was one of those men. He was never able to read, but he was powerful in testimony and prayer.

"Bokari was from the Bozo tribe, making his living poling a boat up the Niger River," Roseberry said. "He was a zealous Muslim, loud-mouthed and ready to fight in an instant. One day pioneer missionaries, Harry and Grace Wright, boarded his boat for a trip up the Niger River that would take fifteen days. Day after day as he poled, his passengers told him of God's plan for his own salvation from sin. He was not yet ready to yield to the call, but he asked to accompany the Wrights on a two-month trip inland two months later. His job was bringing up the rear of the donkey train that carried the baggage. The road was dusty and water was scarce. Bokari had to get the caravan into camp each evening in time to be watered. If he had not been on a quest for God, he would have been tempted to turn back to his former life on the river."

The party reached their destination at Ouagadougou in Upper Volta, and began to build a mission station.

"It was there Bokari won the battle over self and sin," Roseberry continued. "He prayed until his sins were forgiven and the bondage to the flesh was broken. His testimony rang out over a vast area."

"I was a sinner. They called me Bokari the wicked, but the blood of Jesus set me free!" he said.

"He was destined to open citadel after citadel to the gospel in West Africa," Roseberry concluded.

Roseberry took Bokari on one of his annual trips to Timbuctoo in the mission boat, *The Greg.* Bokari was known along the Niger River as "Mona mona" which means "wicked Bokari." When another boatman called him by that name, he would reply, "I am Mona Bokari no longer. I have been saved through Jesus Christ." He gave his testimony everywhere, on the boat, in town or on the river bank. He was tireless in telling the story.

"The restless energy that first drove Bokari to pole boats thousands of miles on the Niger River was now sanctified by God and turned to His own use," Roseberry said. "This man's feet covered trails that stretched from the headwaters of the Niger in the Guinea to Timbuctoo and Gao in the desert and they continued into the forests of the Ivory Coast and back to Guinea."

Wherever he went, men women and children responded to the Gospel. What was his secret? It was **prayer**. He could be heard praying in his hut 'til midnight and early before dawn.

French West Africa was evangelized by men such as Bokari Sava and the list goes on—Julius the Cobbler, Lamin the Nomad, Lai Mara the Gardener, Cova the Pioneer, Sayon the Gold Digger and Tyedian the Farmer—to mention a few. (Their stories are printed in the *Soul of French West Africa* by R. S. Roseberry).

As field director, Roseberry often had to interview representatives from other missions who wanted to open a work in a yet unevangelized area. The French Government required that all new protestant missions be sponsored by the Christian and Missionary Alliance.

After consulting with Mr. Benington, missionary from the Qua Ibo Mission, Roseberry was struck by his vision and fervor.

"You can have the Lobi tribe," Roseberry said.

"As far as I know, they have never heard the gospel."

Benington went to the area of the country now known as Niger and began preaching in the Lobi villages. The Lobi people were perhaps one of the fiercest pagan tribes in West Africa who were adept with the use of the poisoned arrow. They used these arrows to settle all their quarrels before being subdued by the French. One day, a man stepped forward with this strange story.

"For many years I worshipped the gods of my fathers but I was never satisfied. I wondered if their idols could be the true God. Then one day God spoke to me. He told me that He was sending His Word to this place. I burned my fetish in the market place, threw away my bow and arrows and made myself a sword. I put up a red flag at my house. My townspeople didn't like that, so they tied me up hand and foot and threw me out into the field to die. Later they took me before the French Governor, who set me free.

"I waited and waited. Ten years have gone by and now you have come to tell me about the true God," the Lobi tribesman continued. "I believe you are telling the truth. I want to know more about your God."

Always aware of changing times and conditions, Roseberry donned the hat of a strategic planner when he began his last term of service in 1948. He was sensitive to a new spirit of nationalism wafting through Africa and the increasing pressure on colonial powers to grant independence to their colonies. In addition, the administration of such a vast field was becoming unwieldy. Costs for getting missionaries together each year for conference were increasing. As the staff grew, the logistics were staggering. Roseberry felt the time had come for a new innovative approach to getting the task done.

During the 1949 field conference, Roseberry presented his plan for reorganization. The field of French West Africa would become three fields, each with its director, executive committee and conference. It was a hard decision and the consequences difficult to contemplate. It would be like separating a family. Being denied the fellowship and friendship of annual gatherings for conference and vacation was too abrupt a change for a majority to agree. The plan was tabled for more study.

The wisdom of dividing the field became increasingly evident during the following year. By conference time, the missionaries were ready for action. French West Africa became three fields in 1950—Guinea, Ivory Coast and Mali-Upper Volta. It was a providential move because national independence was ushered in all over West Africa by the 1960's. The nightmare of trying to cope with administering the former French West Africa as in pre-independence days was avoided.

With independence, each country set up their

frontier posts with barriers and guards, customs agents and police. Certain ones changed their currencies, most required entry visas, separate I. D. cards and other requirements which complicated travel further. God's leading was in the strategy of dividing into three distinct fields. They were organized and ready for the realities of dealing with newly independent African nations when the time came.

"With the Lord's call for any office goes an anointing of the Spirit. I claimed that promise *"But ye shall receive power, after that the Holy Ghost is come upon you . . ."* (Acts 1:8) and entered the fight with all my soul," Roseberry said. "During my ministry as field director, I count the ministry in the Spirit as the foremost service the Lord granted me to the African Church."

The division of the field also facilitated the organization of the African churches along national lines in later years. It confirmed the importance of being sensitive to the Spirit's leading in strategic planning, discerning the will of . . . *"Him who knows the end from the beginning."* (Isaiah 41:4b NIV)

Chapter 22

THE CLIFF DWELLERS

The vast expanse of wasteland we call the Sahara Desert comes to an abrupt halt before a range of steep cliffs just 200 miles south of Timbuctoo in Eastern Mali. People live there! Their mud and stone villages are erected precariously near the edge of the cliffs or in surrounding gorges. These are the Dogon people, once known as the Habbe tribe.

On a survey trip in the late twenties to Timbuctoo, Roseberry and his party took a side trip into the area. Picture his first encounter with these amazing people.

"At that time the highway zigzagged up over the cliffs. Our Model T Ford didn't go very far before the engine died," Roseberry said. "The gravity-fed carburetor would not dispense gas since the gas tank was lower than the engine! We asked the chief of a nearby village to give us men to pull us up or hold the car back with ropes for the trip back down the cliffs on the other side. Since it was evening when we reached the top, we camped for the night. This was our first contact with the Dogon tribe."

A young couple, Rev. and Mrs. F. W. Foley, were

asked to open up the work among the Dogon people. However, Mr. Foley had contracted tuberculosis while in France during language study and would soon have to return to America.

During the few months they had in Africa, Belko, a young man who worked for them, became convinced of the truth of the gospel and received Christ. He was a Foulani from Mopti and had served 15 years in the French army. He had acquired a knowledge of five or six languages and became a valued interpreter and witness.

Belko had once taken a vow not to shave his head for four years to appease the evil spirits that tormented him. Belko asked to be baptized in a public place and in a sacred moment of the service, he had his head shaved in the name of the Lord Jesus Christ.

"I want everyone to know that I have accepted Christ," he said.

"This endeavor among the Dogon people proved to be fruitful from the very beginning," Roseberry said. "Many of these people turned from dumb idols to serve the living God. The missionaries followed up the new converts with a strong program of instruction. Later, many Dogons went to the central Bible school to become pastors and teachers." *In following years Spirit-filled leaders would emerge among the Dogons who would have an impact on the entire West Africa field.*

The missionary staff began fasting and praying

for a working of God's Spirit when they felt the need for revival in the Dogon Church in the early 60's. Staff members at the time were the Burns, McKinneys and Misses Pond and Battles.

Wageozu Dougnon and Issaka Saye, two young men in their late teens, came in contact with some Mossi Christians from Ouagadougou in Burkina Faso in 1962. The Christians' Spirit-filled lives were a testimony to the young men who immediately wanted to know more, so they put their few belongings on a donkey and set out for Mossi country many miles to their east.

There a young Mossi pastor took them to a church conference. Although they didn't know the Mossi language and couldn't understand the message, they felt the Spirit moving in their lives. An interpreter was called and as they sought God's fullness, they were filled! The next day they were packing their belongings and the pastor asked what they were doing.

"We are going back to our people with the message," the young men quickly replied.

The men told their story when they reached their home village and conviction came on many people. They began to seek the Lord and felt great joy and blessing. These men went from village to village until church after church felt the Spirit's moving. Revival had come! Many lives were touched and these Spirit-filled young men formed teams to go to other districts in other tribes with the same result.

Many of these men became leaders and are currently in various places of authority in the National Churches in West Africa.

One of these men, Pastor Allaye Dougnon, has been leader of the National Church Evangelistic Team in Mali for many years. On his graduation from Bible school, Rev. F. J. McKinney introduced Allaye to Roseberry as a graduate who was beginning his service for Christ.

Roseberry looked intently at him and said, "Young man, you will never amount to anything if you are not filled with the Holy Spirit!"

Allaye said he never forgot the admonition he received that day. A multi-gifted man, he took the message to heart and continues to this day to be a great blessing to many through his Spirit-empowered ministries. The focus of his ministries has been on the importance of the filling of the Spirit for life and service of every believer.

While Pastor Allaye was preaching on a campaign in the Western Mali town of Kayes, a large crowd had assembled in that Islamic center. An elderly Imam from a local mosque stood up to disrupt the message. Suddenly, he began to tremble all over and when he opened his mouth to speak—no sound came from his throat! Humbled and confused, he was helped back to his seat. Everyone perceived this as evidence of God's power working with the witness team. A number were delivered from various diseases and several prayed for salvation during that campaign.

Before an outdoor tent meeting in San, Mali, someone heard a local witchdoctor say the preacher wouldn't last more than 20 minutes. Later, somebody threw a black cat into the large crowd— a witchcraft omen. Thanks to God's protection, nothing happened and God moved in the meeting.

However, when Pastor Allaye undressed for bed that night, a scorpion fell from his pant leg! What praises arose whenever he testified to God's deliverance and how Satan's devices had been defeated!

Christ has given Spirit-anointed leaders to the church in West Africa. They follow in the footsteps of those who led them into the experience of the fullness of the Spirit and taught them how to walk and minister in His power as well.

Chapter 23

PASTORS TRAINED HERE

Roseberry and the Ernest Howards met with prospective students for the new Bible school in a crude shelter made from dried millet stalks fastened to a pole framework. It was not a conference hall, not even an assembly room, but it served as a meeting place in 1936.

Small groups of believers throughout the tribes of French West Africa grew out of wide ranging evangelism by evangelist Bokari Saba. Pioneer missionaries had opened stations, preached and taught. Literacy classes had produced some who could read the few available Scriptures and now it was time to train leaders to pastor churches. But these were married men who had families to support and taxes to pay.

"I was perplexed by the discovery that these men fully expected the mission to support them while in school," Roseberry said. "We could not do that, but hoped they could make farms to support themselves. We decided to call a conference to deepen their spiritual life and promote the training program.

"The Spirit of God came down in that cornstalk

shelter as we preached the Word," he added.

Later Eva Howard recalled Roseberry's message on 'Living Stones' from I Peter 2. He asked the audience to surrender their lives wholly to God and challenged them to become God's building. The sermon moved the hearts of these men so recently converted from idolatry.

"Prayer was answered as men rose from the crude wooden benches and came forward offering themselves for training without reservation," Roseberry said. "In the years ahead students would come from Dogon, Bobo, Senoufo, Mininka, Bambara, Black Bobo and Samogo tribes."

Thus, the Ntorosso Bible School was born, named for the large Bambara village whose chief had donated a field on which an outstation would be built. Services were held under the spreading branches of two huge Baobab trees, because there was no authorization from the government, no buildings and no money in sight.

The shadowy figure of a witch doctor could be seen every day, slinking around during the dark hours as he buried magic charms on the property to hinder the project. But Satan's efforts were foiled. The Ernest Howards were called in from their work among the Foulani at Mopti to take up the challenge and Dr. Oswald Smith, noted pastor and preacher from Canada sponsored the effort. An adobe brick dwelling became the Howard's home and the students themselves erected temporary huts until funds came in so adobe dormitories and outbuildings could be built.

"What great seasons of spiritual blessing we had with the students!" Roseberry remembered. "There were men weeping and seeking the Lord for victory over carnality—others were weeping to be filled with the Spirit. They were going out to battle against great odds and needed the equipment of the early disciples."

That was just the beginning. Later, training centers were built at Telekoro in Guinea, Bouake in the Ivory Coast and Bobo-Dioulasso in Burkina Faso. As education levels increased, a French theological school was started in Yamoussoukro and a seminary in Abidjan, both in the Ivory Coast. Today a host of trained men and women, ordained pastors, evangelists and Christian teachers minister in hundreds of churches large and small throughout West Africa. This is the hope of Africa!

Chapter 24

RIDING ON THE HIGH PLACES

"The field conference of 1951 was very special to Ruth and me for several reasons," Ralph Herber said. "After completing our assignment to learn the Supyire dialect of the Senoufo language and produce a descriptive grammar, we were accepted as senior workers of the French West Africa Mission.

"It was an honor and privilege to join ranks with such a band of heroic missionaries. As the exciting reports of God's working throughout the various areas of the field were given, I had an intense desire to visit the missionaries on their home turf and see for myself what was happening. This opportunity opened to me when I was asked to chauffeur the field director on a field-wide tour.

"It was to be an unforgettable experience, one that provided an opportunity to observe Roseberry's unique approach to ministry close-up. It also expanded my vision and deepened my spiritual life."

By the fifties, converts began to multiply greatly.

"It was physically impossible for me to visit every local church in an area, so we gave much of our time to holding deeper life meetings among them," Roseberry said. "These meetings were short, but they were greatly used of the Lord to deepen the life of the church. For three days we concentrated morning, afternoon and night seeking the Lord and preaching the Word."

"Because of the rapidly increasing numbers of believers, there was a need to move toward organizing the Native Church (later designated National Church)," Ralph continued. "Not only had this policy been mandated by the Christian Missionary Alliance Council, but the events in China in 1949 gave a sense of urgency to move forward toward the goal of establishing self-governing, self-supporting and self-propagating churches all across French West Africa.

"Thus, the goal of this extensive trip was not only to deepen the spiritual lives of the national leaders and believers, but to see flow out of that fresh anointing, the selection of the first national leaders to serve in partnership with the missionary in the oversight of the churches.

"So a few weeks after the conference, following a thorough checkout of our 1947 Chevy Carryall, I left Ruth at Sikasso and drove the 75 miles to meet Dad Roseberry at the airport in Bobo-Dioulasso, in Upper Volta."

"The consciousness of the Lord's presence was

real as we set out from Bobo on June 9," said Roseberry. "We hoped this tour would be the best ever and to this end, committed ourselves to the Lord. The thought 'Riding on the high places' came to mind again and again and so it became our slogan for every station. The Lord made the text, which comes from Deuteronomy 32:13, very real. *'He made him ride on the high places of the earth, that he might eat the increase of the fields and He made him to suck honey out of the rock and oil out of the flinty rock.'* This became our experience throughout the long trip. When we found sickness or discouragement, the cloud lifted and we rode in the high places with the Lord."

"We had not gone very far on the first lap of our tour when one tire blew and another was badly damaged," explained Ralph. "This was serious, because it was almost impossible to purchase tires at that time. An extra spare tire saved us and under the torrid sun, the best tires were switched to the rear. In addition to the heat, a heavy load, including a fifty-gallon drum of gasoline and very rough roads full of pot-holes and deep washboard ridges, made for a challenging gauntlet to run. We committed our way afresh to the Lord and no further tire problems occurred for the rest of the trip.

"We made brief visits at Dedougou among the Red-Bobo tribe and at Sourou among the Maraka and Samogo people. Although only one-night meetings were held, God's blessing was evident as people responded to the Word.

"After devotions following breakfast at Sourou, our hostess, Mrs. Walter Pister, said with a wry smile, 'There's a little visitor to greet us this morning.' We wondered what she meant, then she pointed to the doorway. There, coiled up and motionless, was one of the area's most venomous vipers! A foot-long, drab, mottled olive *'fonfoni'* had crawled under the door right where a person would step. The houseboy quickly dispatched it and we were thankful that none of us had been bitten.

"We left Sourou a little after four, hoping to get a good start because of the long trip ahead. As dawn started to fade the indigo east, we hit wet ground where rain stood from a storm the past night. Later we started to get into more and more sand, which slowed our speed and often required shifting down. We traveled in the glare from the sand-covered landscape for about four hours until at last we arrived within sight of towering rock cliffs which jut abruptly from the sandy plain.

"So this was the land of the Dogon people, West African cliff-dwellers! The amazing sight of a village perched on a high rocky slope soon greeted our light-dazzled eyes.

"At least 200 feet above the road bed were dozens of slate-gray mud and stone houses. They were seemingly fused as an integral part of the congealed lava-like roundness of the mountain. A broken pattern of angular houses and pointed-roof granaries came right up to a straight drop-off.

"After slowly climbing to the plateau above the cliffs, we pulled into Sangha, which was literally built on rock. Comfortable missionary bungalows had been erected using flat slabs of local rock wedged out of the strata of rock stretching in every direction. What a welcome we received from Tom and Delores Burns and the hundreds of Dogon believers and workers gathered there."

"The three-day conference at Sangha in Dogon country stands out as one of the high points of the trip," said Roseberry. "It was the beginning of the farming season and the farmers must take advantage of every gift of moisture to get in their fields of Kafir corn. It took faith and sacrifice for them to leave home and attend the conference as well as hours of slow travel over sandy roads and up the mountain side to the hilltop site of the gathering.

"We were glad to have a good rest before beginning the campaign. It was wonderful to hear the rumble of prayer and intercession ascending toward heaven very early in the morning. The people were seeking God's face in earnest and blessing was assured."

"Dad Roseberry had given me the opportunity to minister the Word and play my accordion as well as be his chauffeur," said Ralph. "In a June 16, 1951 letter to Ruth I said, 'I spoke to the first service, which was a prayer meeting before breakfast. Those men sang so heartily, it was a blessing and a privilege even though I didn't understand their words. That which has been wrought in the hearts of these people has thrilled my heart more than the breath-taking views or the imagination-stirring ruins of ancient cliff-dwellers that attract people to this area.'"

"It was common on such a tour for the African workers to come to me with all sorts of requests," said Roseberry. "There would be a request for added allowance, for help on a wedding dowry, for bicycles, a horse and what not. The head of the mission was supposed to have unlimited power and unlimited resources to meet all their needs!

"We opened our campaign saying we had a favor to ask. 'Do not come to me with any request for three days until the conference is over. Then come.' We wanted the Lord to fill their vision as the great supplier of His people.

"Day after day, we poured out the Word of God and pointed them to the great promises Jesus made to His disciples, *'I will give you a Comforter who shall abide with you forever,'* Much blessing followed the preaching of the Word. They were hungry and wanted to be fed and one meal was not sufficient. Hour after hour, they waited before the Lord.

"Finally the conference drew to a close and not a request for help had come to me, so I sat down with them after the last service. They were seated before me on mats on the floor and I told them to make their requests. All was quiet. Finally, one stood up as spokesman for the crowd. 'Monsieur, we have one request to make. Pray that we may be filled with the Holy Spirit.'

"They kneeled down with their faces to the floor and we joined them as they wept before Him. We prayed that they might be clothed with power from high. What tears were shed! The pools on the mats told the story.

"A committee of five men was chosen by the Dogon conference to help their missionary care for the churches scattered throughout the plains. From that service they filed out and went home to their villages as men who had a vision of the Lord and to win new victories for Him. One of the staff told me it was the dawning of a new day in the work in Dogonland. They went back to their work and we went on our way to the next conference rejoicing in the Lord. We were experiencing the joy of riding on the high places with the Lord."

"The itinerary covered the stations at Dyibasso and Sanekui with the Red Bobos, at Dioundioun with the Minianka people, at the Bible school in Ntorosso among the Bambaras, at Baramba with the Girl's Bible School students and on to conferences in Senoufo country, where Ruth awaited our return," said Ralph. "When we wrote this account, we remembered that some 20 years earlier, yellow fever had taken three of the four missionaries from their labors among the Senoufo tribe. What a joy to have Dad Roseberry visit our house trailer camp in the bush and hold a conference at the out-station of Farakala."

"When the conference began, we had about fifty who gathered from different towns," said Roseberry. "We found open minds and hearts into which we could sow the truth concerning the crucifixion of self on the cross and the pain entailed in surrendering all for Him who suffered so much for us. It came home so deeply that the interpreter stopped and said, 'Eh, that is hard on me!' The deaths of the early pioneers had not been in vain and the Senoufo church had become a reality."

Chapter 25

OIL FROM THE FLINTY ROCK

"After the strenuous weeks of 'riding on the high places' in the Soudan, we again loaded up the Chevy Carry-all," said Ralph. "A couple of days after the Farakala conference, we set our faces toward the Ivory Coast. We prayed God would make us channels of blessing to hungry hearts. Our expectation was that we would *". . . suck oil from the flinty rock"* even as we had experienced *". . . riding on the high places"* earlier.

"As the hours passed, thickening vegetation announced our approach to the great forests of Baouli-land. After seven hours of travel, the weather became cooler and Roseberry slipped on his coat. We arrived in Bouake where it had been raining and were warmly received by Nat and Virginia Billings and Walter Olsen."

"A gathering had been planned including the entire white staff, all the native workers and a number of delegates from the churches in the Ivory Coast's seven districts. When we arrived at Bouake, we found we had several days before the conference, so we arranged to visit as much of the district as

141

possible," said Roseberry. "We lost no time before we set out for Mbayakro and the forest. Mission problems invaded our thoughts and we felt tired and weary with the load. At Mbayakro we were able to pray through and get fresh anointing on our ministry. Ralph Herber ministered with the accordion and in the Word. His messages were effective and his help in prayer and fellowship were a great help in all the conferences."

"The Mbayakro church had no notice of our coming, but they turned out well and gave good attention," said Ralph. "It was refreshing to hear them sing. It is said that the closer one approaches the coast, the better the singing. People in the northern tribes sing the melody in unison, but here they were singing good two- and three-part harmony.

"With the men sitting on the left and the women on the right, they often stood, but at other times, they sang on their knees. The plaintive notes tugged on the soul profoundly as God's forest children worshipped their Savior. We had only one evening with this group before we were off for the new station at Bocanda in the heart of the forest country. Here the Timyans had the responsibility for some 30 district churches, so we decided to visit a town."

"The first night there we were out in the forest ministering at Pokokro," Roseberry said. "This time we rode in the new Jeep. As we penetrated deeper in the forest, we found big mud holes that had been dug out by heavy truck traffic. The Jeep managed to pull

142

through as we went in, but it bogged down in the mud on our way out at night despite its four wheel drive. A line of men with a rope soon put us on our way again. The meeting in the town bore fruit as one young man yielded to the Lord for service and sought the fullness of the Spirit."

"Our faith had been quickened in the afternoon before leaving on the quest for souls, when a distressed-faced believer came for help," Ralph said. "She had been unable to open her mouth for four days and had walked ten miles to be prayed for. Her jaws proved to be indeed tightly clenched."

"She could not explain anything to us, but we and the Timyans laid hands upon her and prayed, demanding that her mouth be opened in the name of Jesus of Nazareth," Roseberry said. "Her mouth was released immediately and she fell on her knees giving praise to the Lord."

"With a look of awe and relief on her face, the woman explained what had happened," continued Ralph. "She had been in the forest cutting wood when a tree she cut fell on a fetish and broke it. The fetish owner demanded a sacrifice to atone for the deed. She was a Christian and refused to obey him and the man became angry and threatened to take her children. She finally escaped with the children only to arrive at her town unable to open her mouth. A curse had been placed upon her. What a wonderful thrill it was to all of us who witnessed her delivery from this evil power in Jesus' powerful name."

"Being thus freed is like coming back from the grave!" she said later.

"Again we had oil out of the rock to pass on to the needy. She went into the district to testify to the power of God in deliverance," said Roseberry.

"We also made brief trips to other districts in the forest country. Dimbokro and the Agni country was our next stop," Ralph said. "We had a great service Sunday morning at Dimbokro where both of us spoke. It ended in a fine altar call and many came seeking the Lord for cleansing. The Lord also brought deliverance to Mr. Joe Ost, one of our Ivory Coast missionaries, who was suffering with a sore back.

"The highlight on this part of the tour was the trip to Tiemelekro, which was accessible only by railroad. We pushed and shouldered our way into an already overcrowded and ancient coach, carrying our filtered water and lunch basket. The most enjoyable part of this train ride was getting off!

"We were soon receiving the greetings of Ibrahima, the chief of this lively Anye church. He was a very old man who was baptized by the prophet, Wade Harris in the mass movement many years earlier. Ibrahima, a short, quick-moving plantation owner with his wrinkled and toothless face had set the pace for the church by his steadfastness and faithfulness in paying the tithe. In honor of the chairman's first visit to his town, Ibrahima presented him with three fine chickens and some rice."

"All three of us preached in the evening service

144

with great acceptance," Roseberry said. "We had to leave about 8:30 a.m. to catch our train back to Dimbokro. The congregation accompanied us to the station and sang gospel songs until the train came in. Old Ibrahima decided that he would attend the conference in Bouake, because he wanted to hear more of the truth of the gospel."

"Roseberry's heart ached for the many believers in districts where the mission lacked personnel. It was depressing to visit empty mission stations and vacant command posts where missionaries had formerly directed the advance into enemy territory," said Ralph. "We prepared lunch in the empty house at Toumodi and then proceeded to visit one of the newest church groups in that district, Soubayakro.

"Winding back through the narrow, tunnel-like forest road past immense trees and impenetrable thickets, we came to the edge of the village clearing where their newly built church stood."

"This group represents a recent victory that began by a young man witnessing on the way to his home town," Roseberry said. "Three young men accepted the Lord who despite beatings, stood true. Later many more were added to the number of believers including the son of the village chief, who had persecuted the young men. A palm leaf-covered arbor had been erected for the short conference, so there was room for all. They gathered from the surrounding district to hear the Word and we had only one night to minister to this fine crowd of believers.

145

Some came for deliverance from the drink habit and there were various other needs. We were sorry we could not stay three or four more days to instruct them more fully in the way of the Lord.

"On our trip back to Bouake for the field-wide conference, we passed through the Tiebissou district without stopping. Our hearts ached with a longing to place someone there to help the struggling churches survive the backfire of heathen worship and the awful drag of the old carnal nature that pulls people back to self-indulgence. If we had campaigned in every church of these three districts even for only one night in each one, it would have required about two months to cover them all."

"Roseberry's heart was stirred again and again as he toured the great forest country and saw the multitudes in the valley of decision," said Ralph. "He had to face the fact that our mission was undermanned, our national pastors few and an abundant harvest unreaped. With such a burden upon him after a fresh anointing of the Spirit, the stage was set for a mighty moving of God at Bouake which would mark a new departure in the work in the Ivory Coast."

"Delegates came in for the conference from every quarter and all the missionary staff was present," Roseberry said. "The twofold object was revival and instruction of the church, leading up to full organization.

"Preparation had been made for months and it

proved to be the best conference ever held in the Ivory Coast. The Lord was with us from the beginning as missionaries were revived opening day when we waited upon the Lord in prayer and with the Word. Joe Ost's messages on the Spirit in the book of Acts were received with joy and the seminar held by Gordon Timyan and others on the organization of the church was excellent. The evangelistic services on the deeper life were very fruitful. There was a great break the second evening and many sought the Lord for victory and the fullness of the Spirit, remaining before Him until the mid-night hour.

"Old Ibrahima was one of the first to break away. He prayed and opened his heart for the Spirit. He stood up with joy and said that the Spirit had come to abide. It was born to our hearts again that the great gaps in the Ivory Coast could be bridged by the moving of the Spirit upon these men who had come. Breathe upon us, oh God, your fullness!"

"The whole conference was marked by a unity of the Spirit and a freshness that greatly lifted us up on the high places with the Lord," said Ralph. "The communion service under the trees was a sacred time of fellowship with the Lord and one another. The election of ten men—five from Upper Ivory Coast and five from Lower Ivory Coast—was an historical occasion which took place in great unity of mind and heart. Their task was to act as an advisory group to the missionary in dealing with church discipline and to help in the dispensing of National Church funds."

"On our return from Bouake we had one evening at Banfora for a service with the believers at Siniena. Hands were raised at the close of the meeting, as they waited for the breath of the Spirit in the Gwen tribe to make them live," said Roseberry. "After a short run to Bobo-Dioulasso and Santidougou we had a prayer meeting with the believers at Bobo and a short conference with the school and church at Santidougou. This ended our tour.

"The Lord's presence was with us both on the highway and in the chapels. May we give thanks to God for His grace and presence as we rode on the high places and shared the honey from the Rock with those who were hungry for God."

"Dad Roseberry boarded a plane and returned to Kankan via Bamako. Ruth, who had stayed at Bobo while we toured the Ivory Coast, joined me for the trip back to Sikasso," said Ralph. "I shared my heartfelt thanks for the great privilege I had experienced being part of such a field-wide tour in a letter to my mother, Ida Herber on July 29, 1951. 'It was a marvelous pleasure and privilege to travel and minister with Dad Roseberry and see what responsibility he carries and has borne for so many years. They will really miss him when he is finished out here.'"

Chapter 26

A TIME FOR REAPING

Browsing through some old copies of the *French West Africa News*, two sentences leapt from the yellow tattered page dated September, 1931. They read, *"It is a pleasure to note that the Lord is working on every station and souls are being saved. In some places there are but one or two while in others many are seeking salvation through the blood of Jesus."*

Page after page told of victories won through toil and sacrifice—of men, women and children in remote areas coming to the missionaries inquiring the way of salvation. The following excerpts are but a few examples of God's Spirit working in French West Africa at that time, leading up to the organization of the National Church a few years later.

SANGHA (Soudan) "We remained at Youdiou five and a half weeks. Five services were held on Sunday. Seventeen villages were visited and thirty-nine prayed for forgiveness of sin. Backsliders were reclaimed and the Christians strengthened. Twenty children were dedicated to the Lord. Tithes and offerings were brought in. Thirty-two followed the Lord in baptism."

BOUAKE (Ivory Coast) "A woman from the

149

Dyimini tribe came to me and said, 'Mister, I am going to my people to tell them about Jesus.' She set off with a sore foot and three weeks later came back after walking all the way. 'I went to my people and they wondered if anyone was going to come tell them how to get to heaven,' she said. She preached in six towns and many knelt and prayed. They pleaded for someone to come help them."

SIKASSO DISTRICT (Soudan) "At one town fifteen men and five boys prayed for forgiveness. One of the men was the village chief and another the owner of many mango trees. When people come to buy mangoes, he tells them about Jesus. On a second visit to teach these believers others also turned to the Lord ."

SAN (Soudan) "Work among boys at the French-speaking school (started by Ethyl Bell) is progressing rapidly. Their number has increased to fifty-seven. While witnessing in his heathen town, one of the boys won fourteen of his townspeople to the Lord. Eight of the boys were baptized during Mr. Roseberry's visit."

MBAYAKRO (Ivory Coast) "The church at Mbayakro, under the leadership of Moise, is flourishing. The chapel, which was erected a year ago, was crowded at every service. The believers have more than doubled and eleven were baptized. After the worship service they have a prayer meeting that continues far into the night. The sick are prayed for and every need held up to God."

SAN (Soudan) When we arrived in San we found

workers preparing for one of the greatest conferences this field has seen. Ninety-seven delegates came from nineteen towns. Many rose and told how the Lord had reached them and delivered them from their fetish worship. Old gray-haired men, who a few months before had not known anything but fetish worship, called mightily on God in prayer. For three days they were taught about new Life in Christ."

NTOROSSO (Soudan) "An excellent work has been done there. By perseverance, even during the farming season, many had mastered the new primers and were reading in the New Testament. People came almost daily from far and near to repent and ask workers to come to their town so they could burn their fetishes. This was first done in great fear, but their fear was replaced by joy as they heaped their weird charms on the fire. They have been called from darkness into the Light."

BOCANDA (Ivory Coast) "Twenty-five followed the Lord in a baptismal service even though the stream was shallow and muddy for this time of year. The service was a precious one. At communion service the church was filled. Row after row came until nearly two-hundred had partaken of the emblems, showing faith in His death until He shall come."

BEOMI (Ivory Coast) "A movement began in this section during the past year. There were many decisions for Christ. Albert, one of the workers, has gone to be with Christ, but his wife has won seven women to the Lord. When word was sent for Christians to gather, about one-hundred fifty responded. We hope to build a mission station there soon."

KISSI TRIBE (Guinea) "Workers are now occupying four counties in Kissiland. The people respond in every town. Mr. Robert Adam preached from under an umbrella in a drizzle and when the invitation was given, forty-nine responded. The night before in another town, thirty-four came for prayer."

Only eternity will reveal why the reaping began in such evident ways a few months after the 1931 deaths of missionaries to yellow fever in Sikasso. It was thought by some missionaries, including Roseberry, that the shock of those losses may have raised up great intercession for the beleaguered corps of workers as well as prayer against the powers of darkness holding the tribes in bondage to Satan. It is a matter of record that missionaries, as well as homeland supporters, cried mightily to God during those testing days. Psalm 126:5-6 seems to describe it well. *"Those who sow in tears will reap with songs of joy. He who goes out weeping carrying seed to sow, will return with songs of joy carrying sheaves with him."*

Chapter 27

STATESIDE INTERLUDES

In the early days of mission penetration in French West Africa, missionaries spent four years at their post, followed by a year in their homeland. This was called a furlough. It was a time for rest and renewal, but also an opportunity to speak in churches all over the United States and Canada, telling of God's working on the field. Roseberry considered this a challenge and a privilege.

As one such furlough came to a close, however, events took a different turn. It was the fall of 1941. After Pearl Harbor and other events of World War II, all travel on the Atlantic had come to a halt. The Roseberrys could not return as planned, so when a request from Simpson Bible School came for him to teach missions, he readily accepted. Edith chose to stay in the apartment at Taylor University where Ruth was in her senior year. Though separation was never easy, entering open doors for ministry and putting the work of the Kingdom ahead of personal advantage had become a way of life with the Roseberrys.

After thirty-two years of ministry in West Africa,

it was strange to be on a college campus in America! In the beautiful setting of the the Pacific Northwest, Roseberry rejoiced in the opportunity to light a flame for God and impart the vision that had animated his service. "Mr. and Mrs. J. D. Williams, who were in charge of the school, desired to keep the school on a revival level. My aim was to lift the school to a missionary level," Roseberry said.

"He made an impression on every student. He entered into school life, tossed horseshoes with the fellows and spent time with the students in any way he could," said a former student. "He had a special interest in those 'big fellows from Alaska' and I am sure he wanted them in French West Africa."

The brothers Nate and Joe Ost, along with their wives eventually did serve many years with him in Guinea and the Ivory Coast. Dick and Barbara Lytle were also touched for ministry through his life and also served as missionaries in Guinea.

"Furlough time in the States always presented a new challenge to me," said Roseberry. "My motto was *'Seek a new elevation.'* During what is now called home assignment, he was often invited to speak at summer Bible conferences of The Christian and Missionary Alliance such as at Mahaffey, Pennsylvania; Delta Lake, New York; Beulah Beach, Ohio and others.

"At the Mahaffey Convention in 1928, a deep impression came to arrange for a special prayer hour for missions," he said. "The only available hour was from 8-9 a.m., but we were delighted to see some prayer warriors there. Mr. D. J. Fant, Sr. and Mrs. J. D. Williams and others prayed earnestly for the needs of the fields as presented. As a result, the hour of intercession became a regular part of that convention." Roseberry was also successful in setting up an intercession hour in other summer camps where he was called to minister through the years.

While at Winona Lake Conference, Roseberry made contact among the Mennonite Holiness people in Indiana and they asked him to speak at their annual convention near Goshen. "Special missionary intercession was new to them. They had missionary money, but few candidates to send to the field," he said. "They soon became conscious that much was lacking in their experience. It hit one brother so hard that he broke down and kneeled in prayer confessing his need. Later when my wife gave her testimony, a great number came forward for prayer."

Later while attending a conference at Delta Lake, Roseberry received God's healing touch. The well-known Alliance evangelist, Rev. W. G. Weston, was the speaker. While he was praying, God revealed to him that Roseberry had a need.

"I looked him up in his tent and found him waiting for me," Roseberry said. "I told him of a serious need in my body that would hinder me from carrying the heavy load awaiting me in Africa. That man of God put his arms around me and prayed for my full deliverance and the work was done!" Symptoms didn't cease at once, but just as it happened to the lepers Jesus touched, ". . . *as they went they were cleansed.*" The healing touch of Jesus was a reality!

Once while on tour in Los Angeles, California, evangelist Armin Geswein came to see Roseberry and a friendship in the Lord was born that endured through the years. "He wanted to join forces with me in evangelism and I felt it to be the will of God," Roseberry said. "Our first campaign was in a Baptist church in Elkhart, Indiana. We were both strong on having a daily Bible study and time of intercession. The pastor feared his people wouldn't come, but what days of heart-searching and prayer we had! The meetings went on for four weeks instead of two. An elder fled to the prayer room after one message. One lady was filled with the Holy Spirit as she lay on her bed at night." During six weeks of ministry Roseberry felt he had a new horizon and a new elevation in the hope of revival kindled in his heart that would affect his ministry ever after.

Chapter 28

KNIGHT OF THE LEGION OF HONOR

Some thirty-two years had passed since the small band of workers under the leadership of Roseberry began their penetration of French West Africa to build the Church of Christ. The Christian and Missionary Alliance was the first Protestant Mission to be granted permission to go into the interior of the country. The government was at a loss to know how to fit it into their laws. There were endless negotiations and yards of red tape and the French officials secretly hoped the missionaries would grow weary of it all and go home.

But they underestimated the God-given call of the early pioneers. Even though they faced false reports by antagonistic enemies, missionaries went quietly ahead and made friends with many, including some officials. By 1952, there had been real gains and French West Africa was dotted with mission stations, chapels, schools and groups of believers coming from many tribes and language groups.

Roseberry was honored by the French Government on December 5, 1952—a day long to be remembered. "Movie cameras were grinding away when the Governor of the Colonies, with a new cap for the occasion, marched forward to face me. The crowd in Guinea's capitol Conakry, included a color guard and local officials," Roseberry said. "After a few words, the governor touched me on both shoulders and pinned the Knight of the Legion of Honor medal on my coat. He kissed me on both cheeks as was the French custom. Then my dear wife, so timid and shy, came forward and kissed me, followed by congratulations from Dr. A.C. Snead our Foreign Secretary and Mr. Gerig of the Missionary Church Association."

As his fellow workers came forward to congratulate him, Roseberry felt strongly that the honor also belonged to them, because they had joined him in the long struggle to make Christ known to many tribes. They had gone through deadly epidemics of yellow fever and had suffered many privations in their search for living jewels. In the early days they had been maligned and troubled in their quest, but now they were being recognized and honored through their beloved leader. The recognition of Protestant Missions that day marked a new epoch in the development of the relationship between missions and the government. Roseberry had been the catalyst in the formation of the Federation of Missions. Its basic structure would be replicated in each of the former colonies after they acquired independence from France in the years 1958-1960. Only eternity will reveal the breadth of impact this development is still having, over forty years later.

Chapter 29

NEW HORIZONS

Who could ever forget the sun setting over the rippling waters of Lake Erie at the close of day? This pleasant area became the retirement home of the Roseberrys in 1953. An inheritance from a beloved sister, Annie Kinch, had made possible a comfortable home at Beulah Beach, Ohio before their last term in West Africa.

"The beach is a lovely place in spring and summer. Summer conferences held there provide the best in preaching and missionary information," said Roseberry. "The lake offers swimming and fishing to help one relax and rest. Garden land can be rented where one can vie with another in raising the biggest tomatoes, corn and cucumbers and patches of blackberry plants are nearby. One can drive for miles through the countryside past vast fruit farms."

Forty-four years had passed since Roseberry entered West Africa. He had spearheaded the entry of the gospel into French Soudan and its neighbors of Guinea, Upper Volta and the Ivory Coast. Now it was time to retire and pass the torch on to others.

Returning to the states to stay in 1953, they were

soon settled in—happy among many friends who also lived on the grounds. For six years, it was only a headquarters for Roseberry as he continued to minister in missionary conferences or deeper life meetings in churches. At seventy-two years of age he was blessed with abundant health. Two years after settling at the beach, he was able to take a five-month tour in West Africa. During that time he spoke in about thirty conferences with the African Church and missionaries.

But retirement did not mean the end of ministry. "For a number of years Mrs. Roseberry was able to minister to the sick and needy," Roseberry said. "Sometimes she would stay with the sick through the night. It was her delight to help. Our home was open for the sick to come for prayer. A Baptist brother came with his wife who was ill. I anointed the lady and my wife prayed earnestly until the Spirit of God witnessed to her heart that the work was done. My wife was quiet and humble, giving all the glory to God."

Whether at Beulah Beach or at subsequent retirement homes, conducting Bible studies was an important ministry. "A door soon opened to me to minister to the saints. I found many hungry hearts waiting to receive the deep things the Lord had taught me through the years," Roseberry explained after their move to the Alliance Home in Carlisle, Pennsylvania. "As I taught with a new abandonment to the Lord, the Word was opened to me with fresh

162

The "missionary family" gathers together for Annual Conference at Kankan, mid-1930s.

Two friends and pioneer collaborators: Roseberry and Harry Wright.

Roseberry with grandson Robert Herber during one final visit to West Africa in 1955.

The Roseberrys retire to the home the Lord provided in Beulah Beach, Ohio.

Furlough time reunites Roseberrys with their four grandchildren: Robert, Sharon, Edward and Patricia Herber.

Roseberry alone in his room in the Alliance Home at Carlysle, Pennsylvania, after Edith's homegoing in 1964.

In 1967, Roseberry is wed to Mrs. Anne German. They moved to DeLand, Florida in 1968.

revelation of the Spirit. It was an artesian well flowing all the time. We have not yet seen the full fruit of our labors, but we press on. Our chief desire is to raise up a band of praying warriors who will reach the ends of the earth."

Sometimes my father got a bit frustrated in his zeal to see action. "I just can't seem to get these old folks stirred up to pray for missions," he said in a letter to us. He did not identify with his peers, because in his late eighties, his vigor was being renewed day by day. He also traveled daily through the mission fields by prayer and thoughts. This was a ministry that continued most of his remaining days on earth. We were always conscious of his prayers for us, his children and for the great Senoufo people we were trying to reach for Christ.

After his move to Deland, Florida, when he was 90 years old, he was asked to give a missionary charge to Timothy Hixon on the occasion of his ordination.

"I had not stood up to speak for two years," Roseberry said. "By Sunday noon my voice was weak. After dinner I lay down and slept a while and prayed, looking to the Lord for strength and unction. By seven I was on the platform and ready for action. I was introduced after a long program and I stood before a full house and delivered the message to all. My legs were like new and my voice strong and full. What a service! I believe the Lord spoke to many. It was like riding on angel wings."

163

Chapter 30

ADRIFT ON LAKE ERIE

"Roseberry and two of his neighbors at Beulah Beach Bible Conference had been offered a speedy motorboat, so they set out to fish on Lake Erie on a pleasant balmy day in June of 1960," said Ralph. "As the afternoon started to wane, a brisk wind sprang up, a forerunner perhaps, of some ominous dark clouds in the distance. When they attempted to crank up the engine, it wouldn't fire. Now a strong wind was taking the small Plexiglas boat out into the lake. Again and again they tried to start the engine without success. Plainly they were in trouble and the cement block used for an anchor did not prevent them from drifting farther and farther from shore.

"Night came and although they never lost sight of lights on the shore and the water tower at Vermillion, Ohio, the boat and its alarmed occupants could not be seen. The boat owner, Millen Nussbaum, got another boat and looked for them and other boats joined in the search along with a plane and helicopter. No sign of the drifting men was discernible in the midst of the turbulent waves.

"As the billows began to mount higher and

165

higher, the men crouched under the cowl in the prow. It was very crowded, but by crouching and using the life preservers, they had partial protection from the rain. Five different thunderstorms beat upon them throughout the night. After each downpour, they bailed out the water. Remarkably, though soaked, they did not chill. It was a time of heart-searching and counting the cost as the hours slowly went by.

"As the boat drifted across the lake, the men prayed and waited for the dawn. On shore the weather bureau was predicting a tornado and the clouds reflected an ominous light. The Coast Guard was making every effort to find them, but to no avail.

"Edith Roseberry stood on the bank overlooking Lake Erie at 4:30 p.m., lifting her heart to the Lord. As she prayed, the presence of the Lord surrounded her like a mantle and lifted her spirit into a state of repose and calm that took away all fear. She went home and slept, peaceful in the assurance that God was in control. Mrs. Klein, wife of one of the men, also went to bed and slept. As the night wore on and prayer groups were praying for deliverance, David Clark, the district superintendent stayed near his phone all night, waiting for a call. News of three men lost on the lake was flashed over the radio and published by the press."

"About 3 a.m. hope was running low, because the storm was still raging around us. Then there came a flash of hope," said Roseberry. "A Capitol Airline pilot on his way from Detroit to Atlanta, was flying slightly off course when he spotted our tiny signal light that we had connected by wire to the steering post. The pilot had heard of our plight over the radio and immediately sent word to the airport fixing the position of our boat. The Coast Guard had stopped the search because of the stormy conditions and darkness. Now they went into action again, mapping out the lake in sections. Eventually they spotted our little flashing light. They homed in on it and we soon heard the chug-chug of the engine as they approached our tossing craft."

"The big spotlight of the Coast Guard boat picked up the form of the boat and drew alongside. Deliverance had come just before dawn," Ralph said. "The men crawled from their cramped quarters under the cowl, their wet bodies stiff from the long hours of being huddled together. The young men from the Coast Guard were met by a hearty, 'Praise the Lord!' and they soon had the men wrapped in warm blankets drinking cups of hot coffee. It had been a long night for all concerned.

"The news of the rescue was flashed to Beulah Beach and the night vigils of prayer turned into outpourings of rejoicing and praise."

"Newspaper reporters vied with each other to get the scoop for their papers," Roseberry said. "There were pictures, interviews and questions."

"How could unbelieving men understand the care

167

of our Almighty God for His servants?" asked Ralph. "Could it have been mere chance that a well trained commercial pilot went off course or that he was constrained to scan the inky blackness beneath him and be attracted to one small blinking light that shouldn't be there? For the three men it was not a question 'if' God could deliver them, but 'when?'

"The Lord had not forgotten to be gracious and hear the cry of His servants and the host of intercessors in their behalf," said Roseberry. "Oh, that men would praise the Lord for His goodness to the children of men!"

Chapter 31

A GODLY HERITAGE

Children were a joy to my father. He played with them, told them stories and prayed for them! When the cable arrived telling of his first grandson's private invasion of the world on D-Day, 1944, it was a special time. Because he was back in Africa, he would not see Robert, his namesake, for two more years, but weekly letters showed his love and concern. He lived to see three more grandchildren, Sharon Ruth, born in 1951, Ralph Edward, born in 1955 and Patricia Anne, born in 1957. Circumstances prevented his being with them a lot through the years, but there were those precious times when furloughs brought all the family together.

The children of missionaries often don't know their grandparents very well because of the many years of living far away in a distant land. For that reason, our furlough years of 1958 and 1963 were spent living near Mother and Dad Roseberry. Beulah Beach was a fun place to live—sandy beaches along Lake Erie, good fishing when the white bass were running and lots of activities for the children. When Ralph was away on missionary tours, Grandpa Roseberry had fun times with the grandchildren.

When she was seven years old, Sharon loved to go berry picking with grandpa in the summer time in a tangled berry patch across the highway. Picnics, birthdays and holidays were special. It was always hard to say good-bye at year's end and it was with mixed feelings that we returned to our African home. Leaving our son, Bob stateside in 1959 was very hard, but knowing his godly grandfather would be there for him was a comfort. Father was proud of his grandson's accomplishments.

Father lived to see two of his six great-grandchildren. Wende, Bob's eldest daughter, was the first. Father took the infant in his arms and dedicated her to the Lord. Jamie, daughter Pat's first born, would never remember when her parents took her to see her great-grandfather and how he prayed for her when she was less than a year old. Some day we trust each of them will realize the heritage they have in such a special servant of the Lord.

As father's physical strength began to wane, his spirit turned more to prayer and writing articles and letters of encouragement. After a move to Deland, Florida in 1969, home was an apartment on the fifteenth floor of the College Arms towers, a senior citizen high-rise building in Deland, Florida. I can still see him in his favorite arm chair in front of the picture windows, looking out to the East, over the coast of Florida.

You could see that far away look in his eyes and know he was again walking the trails of West Africa. There beyond the horizon an ocean away, lay a land he loved with throngs of as yet unreached people whom he longed to see around the throne of God worshipping the Lamb one day. He would pray for Africans he knew by name, for the church going through its growing pains and he would intercede for the missionary staff and the need for more workers.

Father's prayers and encouragement followed us during twenty-nine years of our career in West Africa. He typed letters regularly as long as he could, including nuggets of truth from his gleanings of the Word. Later when typing was difficult, he sent messages of counsel, encouragement and love through his wife. We still have the packet of letters he handed us as we boarded the S. S. America for our voyage to France in 1947. He told us we were to open them later—one for each day of the trip. What an inspiration they were then and still are even forty-nine years later! The testings and trials we encountered were faced with confidence because we knew he was praying.

172

Chapter 32

THE LAST FRONTIER

My mother was the first to cross that last frontier into the presence of the Lord. Her physical condition had deteriorated while we were in Africa. So in order to be near my parents during our furlough in 1963-64, we again decided to look for a rental opportunity at Beulah Beach. During our year there, we could see mother's strength failing. Father was doing the house work and caring for her and he realized they would need to go to a place where she could have special care.

When time came for us to return to the field, we prayed as a family and good-byes were exchanged. We had the feeling that our next meeting with mother would be in heaven. A few weeks after our return to Mali, word arrived telling of their move to Carlisle, Pennsylvania. Kind friends helped them pack and drove them to the Alliance Home and settled them into a small apartment.

However, the message also contained sad news. Rising from a nap that same evening and forgetting that a door in the hall opened to a flight of stairs into the basement, mother unfastened the door and

173

plunged down the steps and broke her leg. She had good care and seemed to improve, but her frail body couldn't stand the shock. She was eighty-five years old. Two weeks later she left for that city where all is peace and there is no more pain. Our oldest son, Robert and his wife represented us at the funeral.

Well into our fourth term in Mali, father's well-being became a concern. It seemed unlikely that he could be happy in his small room in the Alliance Home. We wondered if we should leave our ministry in Africa to provide a home for him, since I was the only child. However, I also knew that he would not want us to leave our work. God had the answer for us all.

Mrs. Anne German, widowed and also a former pastor, was working in the home's business office. A close friendship grew to engagement and marriage. Together they joined their gifts in an effective ministry. During our furlough in 1968, we moved them to Deland, Florida. Before we returned to Mali, Dad laid his hands on our two teen-agers heads and committed Ed and Pat to the Lord.

Dad and Anne were happy in their high-rise apartment. They had a weekly Bible class for residents and enjoyed the ministries of First Alliance Church where she played the organ. They later moved to a retirement center in Altoona, Florida. The weight of advancing years took their toll and Dad's strength waned. Anne cared for him lovingly until July, 1976 when he too, crossed that last frontier to the welcoming presence of Christ. We are deeply grateful to her.

When Ralph visited him in May of that year during an unexpected trip to the States, father told him to take a last message to the African Church for him. It was simply Acts 1:8 *"You shall receive power after the Holy Spirit has come upon you. And you shall be my witnesses . . . ."* Father slipped away to meet his Lord at five o'clock in the morning as he had done in prayer throughout his long life.

As I was preparing this manuscript, a copy of the *French West Africa Quarterly News* was sent to me. It contained this tribute to Roseberry at the time of his retirement in 1953. *"The French West Africa Mission of the Christian and Missionary Alliance desires to express its gratitude for the Herculean task accomplished by the man who has been its chairman these many years. No one knows missions in French West Africa as does R. S. Roseberry. He alone holds the blue ribbon for travel by river boat, automobile and airplane from the Northern Dogon plains to the forests of the Ivory Coast, from the 4,000-foot Djallon mountains to the easternmost Upper Volta station hundreds of miles away.*

"Mr. Roseberry knew African missionary labors in their most primitive form. On the other hand, he has been one of Africa's most progressive persons in campaigning for improvements, advancement and completion of the task remaining. The Christians of French West Africa will be eternally grateful for

Robert S. 'Roseberry's godly life, in bringing the Light to their land."

Father was also a godly influence in our own lives and a great encouragement and prayer partner. He touched countless others in life-changing ways. Whether teaching in Bible College or ministering in churches, young people were challenged to give their lives for the Lord's work. I have met a few— a pastor in Wisconsin, a missionary couple from another mission, a faithful lay worker in a church, a career missionary in South America and many others. Some were influenced as children when he was entertained in their homes. Though we weren't able to join those who laid him to rest, we remember him as we last said good-bye and treasure the many memories of a father who was a true "Man of God," In a lifetime that spanned over 90 years, he was not *". . . disobedient to the heavenly vision."*

BIBLIOGRAPHY

Crossing Frontiers With Christ.
Unpublished autobiography of Rev. R. S.
Roseberry, 1958.

The Niger Vision.
R. S. Roseberry, Christian Publications, Harrisburg,
PA, 1934.

Among the Cliff Dwellers of French West Africa.
Rev. and Mrs. F. J. McKinney and R. S. Roseberry,
The Christian and Missionary Alliance, 1936.

West Africa Field News.
Kankan, Guinea, West Africa, 1931.

Personal family letters of Herbers and Roseberrys.

The Soul of French West Africa.
R. S. Roseberry, Christian Publications, Harrisburg,
PA 1947.

West Africa Witness.
Kankan, Guinea, West Africa, 1953.